WALK YOUR TALK

Tom

Thanks for your support and for being so generous with your time.

WALK YOUR TALK

MAKING SENSE OF LEADERSHIP

TED MCKINNEY, PHD

MANUSCRIPTS
PRESS

WALK YOUR TALK
Making Sense of Leadership

ISBN   979-8-88926-246-6   *Paperback*

979-8-88926-247-3   *Hardcover*

979-8-88926-245-9   *Ebook*

This book is dedicated to my parents.
Without your support, this achievement
would have been impossible.

CONTENTS

INTRODUCTION

When people think about the role of a leader, they often focus on defining strategy, making tough decisions, and ensuring the company is profitable. While those are good bullet points for a job description, leadership is primarily about the signals leaders send and how employees understand them.

One morning, our cleaning person, Beth, approached me. It was during a trying time in my life. In addition to running a twelve-doctor, twenty-four-seven veterinary clinic, my wife was pregnant, I was in the early stages of a PhD program, and my father was fighting terminal cancer. Beth handed me a doctor's note and apologized for missing work the previous day. I thanked her and explained that the note needed to go to our human resource manager.

She knew that protocol but said, "I just thought you were mad at me for calling off."

Usually, I said good morning to her, but I'd broken our routine that day. Beth didn't know how to interpret the omission of my morning greeting. She assumed intent—that my disregard was premeditated. I was sleep-deprived, overwhelmed, and engrossed in thoughts about Dad's deteriorating health. I wasn't aware Beth had missed work, and that morning, I was unaware of Beth.

She, however, was keenly aware of my detachment. Beth was alarmed that I had not spoken to her. As she processed cues from her environment, she formed a reality where my behavior was related to her previous day's absence.

When a leader leaves a blank to make sense of, self-preservation often leads to employees filling it in with something more sinister than reality. How can leaders create an environment where Beth can safely say, "Hey, boss, is something wrong? Are you mad at me?"

This process of framing experiences is called sensemaking. It is "how we structure the unknown so as to be able to act in it."[1] What is a leader's role in how employees make sense of their world?

Leaders are always on stage.

Body language is never silent.

Silence is never silent.

Leaders must be strategically aware of verbal and nonverbal communication and behaviors. Philosopher and scholar Mikhail Bakhtin said, "Language, for the individual consciousness, lies on the borderline between oneself and the other. The word in language is half someone else's."[2] As a result, communication relies on the receiver's interpretation of the message, and the lens of their past experiences always clouds that interpretation.

Therefore, reality is a function of how we interpret people's words, deeds, and other environmental signals. The challenge is that everyone assumes their framing represents the truth rather than merely a unique subjective experience influencing how they perceive the world.

In a work setting, a leader's behavior is the primary sensemaking input employees use. Researchers have explained this phenomenon as "the shadow of the leader."[3]

Over time, sensemaking evolves from an individual's impression to a collective understanding. This shared meaning becomes the foundation of the work culture. Grasping this is crucial because the work culture can stand between business strategy and business results.

Edgar H. Schein suggested, "because culture constrains strategy, a company must analyze its culture and learn to manage within its boundaries or, if necessary, change it."[4] The salient point is that culture limits the kinds of strategies that leaders can execute.

Leadership is contextual, enigmatic, and evolving. Consider this definition from a 1927 management conference that defined leadership as "the ability to impress the will of the leader on those led and induce obedience, respect, loyalty, and cooperation."[5] Contrast that with a more recent assessment of leadership that concludes, "Leaders are one element of an interactive network that is far bigger than they."[6]

How can a leader know how to behave if everything is circumstantial, and employees' needs and preferences are capricious?

For example, most people do not want authoritative leaders. However, directive leadership facilitates team functioning in circumstances like emergency rooms or when responding to a crisis.[7] In these situations, people benefit from removing ambiguity, providing structure, and satisfying a need for predictability and security.

On the opening weekend of my doctoral program, Dr. Amy C. Edmondson—Novartis professor of leadership and management at Harvard Business School, who has long studied the performance of teams in the workplace— spoke about psychological safety. She defines it as "a shared belief held by members of a team that the team is safe for interpersonal risk taking."[8] As I listened, I began to wonder if psychological safety was the remedy for the toxicity I had experienced. The inspiration evolved into a question I knew was worthy of research: What is the relationship between leadership behaviors and employees' perceptions of psychological safety?

In these pages, I share my research and the studies, experiences, and stories that led to my paradigm shift. Thriving organizations and thriving employees are not mutually exclusive. A psychologically safe work culture promotes employee well-being and enhances organizational productivity. But...

Psychological safety has an image problem. Many assume it is coddling, kowtowing to employees, or a byproduct of a "woke agenda." Elon Musk, one of the most accomplished and controversial people of the twenty-first century, is renowned for setting ambitious goals and working tirelessly to achieve them. He is a demanding leader and an example of the misconceptions about psychological safety.

In *Elon Musk*, Walter Isaacson wrote, "Musk let loose a bitter laugh when he heard the phrase 'psychological safety.' It made him recoil. He considered it to be the enemy of urgency, progress, orbital velocity. His preferred buzzword was 'hardcore.' Discomfort, he believed, was a good thing. It was a weapon against the scourge of complacency."[9]

Musk's sentiment sounds like what I believed a decade ago, but it is antithetical to my understanding of leadership today.

Social psychologist Douglas McGregor states, "The motivation, the potential for development, the capacity for assuming responsibility, the readiness to direct behavior toward organizational goals are all present in people. Management does not put them there. It is a responsibility of management to make it possible for people to recognize and develop these human characteristics for themselves."[10]

Research shows psychologically safe cultures are the key to unleashing this potential.

Gallup reports that employee disengagement may cost the economy $1.9 trillion.[11] Research shows creating a psychologically safe culture decreases turnover and positively affects communication, innovation, creativity, collaboration, empowerment, engagement, and learning from failure. In other words, psychological safety is not just good for employees; it fosters performance that benefits the bottom line!

Walk Your Talk will help executives, managers, board members, or psychological safety enthusiasts appreciate and capitalize on the relationships between leadership behaviors, employee sensemaking, work culture, and organizational success. This book provides an evidence-based model leaders can follow to foster a healthy work culture, employee well-being, and team performance.

The following chapters will review several case studies from organizations that have adopted different leadership approaches based on their unique context. We will investigate the factors that promote or inhibit psychological safety. What worked, what didn't, and why? You will:

- Peek behind the curtain at an organization that has grown to $3.3 billion in annual revenue by focusing on its employees. CEO Bob Chapman's belief that culture can be a competitive advantage directly reflects Barry-Wehmiller's guiding principle: "We measure success by the way we touch the lives of people."[12] Examining

Barry-Wehmiller's culture will help you understand the link between a culture emphasizing employee well-being and organizational performance.

• Consider what may have happened with Boeing's leadership in 2020 when planes began falling out of the sky. Did the breakdown happen decades earlier because of a culture shift where safety and quality became subservient to profit? What, if anything, could have been done to prevent the tragedies?

• Learn from a retired Air Force colonel about the role psychological safety played throughout his career and why sacrificing for others is central to effective leadership in the military. He reflects on his time as a cadet at the Air Force Academy, in the cockpit of an F-15 fighter jet, as an operating group commander with more than twenty-seven hundred airmen reporting to him, and as a FedEx pilot of a Boeing 777 on transatlantic flights.

Supportive, purpose-driven cultures build momentum and reinforce themselves over time. Roles and expectations are clear, and being held responsible for what you control is expected. People learn from failure; it does not define them. The environment becomes safe for risk-taking, so an individual's need for self-preservation does not prevent them from contributing to the organization's goals. Unlike the anxiety-inducing "discomfort" Musk advocates for, employees feel a sense of acceptance, inclusion, and belonging that allows them to engage fully.

CHAPTER 1:

A RELATIONAL MODEL FOR LEADING

"The only thing of real importance that leaders do is to create and manage culture. If you do not manage culture, it manages you, and you may not even be aware of the extent to which this is happening."

—EDGAR H. SCHEIN

My best employment experiences have always resulted from good working relationships with my bosses. That seems like a self-evident statement, but a Gallup statistic emphasizes its importance: 70 percent of employee engagement results from the employee's relationship with their manager.[1]

AFFIRMATION

As my evolution from a top-down to a bottom-up leader progressed, an experience affirmed the relational leadership philosophy I had been contemplating. At the end of 2021—during the COVID-19 pandemic—I joined a nonprofit behavioral health organization as its executive director.

One counselor described the mission as "a model for equity in mental health." She illustrated her point using two cases.

1. A single mother of four, working at Walmart, paid fifteen dollars weekly for therapy.
2. An affluent family with a teenage son in therapy paid one hundred and sixty-five dollars a session.

Both clients receive the same quality care from her each week. She explained that without the organization subsidizing low-income clients, the single mom would likely not get help, or, if lucky, an overworked clinician at another agency who did not have the time or resources to invest in her would put her on a waitlist.

The nonprofit had served the community for over fifty years but was steeply declining. The pandemic exacerbated the problems. The board brought me in to identify the root causes of the decline and develop and implement a turnaround plan.

In 2019, the organization lost its long-time executive director, and the subsequent director lasted less than a year. The development director also resigned in my first year. In the leadership churn, relationships with donors, employees, and the board deteriorated. Board recruitment and engagement suffered. It got to the point that we had to rewrite our bylaws to ensure a meeting quorum.

Employee turnover resulted in a 50 percent drop in clinical revenue, and during the two years that preceded my arrival, the center lost almost half of its donor base. The agency barely broke even my first year thanks to $300,000 in forgiven PPP loans. Our *equity in mental health* model created a fundraising challenge to subsidize our sliding scale fee structure. The more "mission" work the center did, the more of a fundraising burden it created.

We paid clinicians a commission, but this compensation structure harbored competing values. A clinician's compensation for a low-income client, even with our subsidy, was a fraction of what they earned from someone with insurance or paying the full fee out of pocket.

I explained to the board that the staff primarily fell into two groups. Many of the clinicians who had resigned were "capitalists," willing to support the mission but defensive of it impacting their pocketbooks. Most who remained were "altruists," bearing the brunt of the mission at a high personal cost.

A lack of transparency during the leadership churn muddled the collective understanding of the broader mission. For example, I remember sitting with a therapist who explained they perceived insurance clients as part of the "mission" because many local counselors no longer accepted insurance.

All stakeholders should have a common understanding of goals, and the confusion about our mission was a symptom of the organization's relational deterioration. For some on the board, the narrative became about greedy clinicians running "private practices" because they would not see subsidized clients. The "capitalists" were not greedy. They were playing by the established rules. Many were simply trying to meet their basic financial needs.

The clinical staff was on the front lines of a second mental health pandemic. The crisis was overwhelming. I remember being told, "You have no idea what it's like to listen to people cry eight hours a day." Compassion fatigue and burnout were inescapable for the staff. Social distancing had limited the type of support we could provide. The staff wanted more help but could not identify tangible actions that would meet their needs. Multiple people said, "Where's the board?" Most of them just wanted to be heard and understood. They wanted a relationship.

I could empathize with the relational vacuum they felt. Most staff still saw clients remotely from offsite locations. I found it challenging to build trust and relationships without the informal interactions that would typically happen in the hallways or the breakroom. I was there for months before I met some of the counselors. Without the connections, it often felt like I was managing things, not leading people.

END OF THE LINE

Ultimately, we needed more resources, time, and bandwidth to execute a turnaround. The center joined a larger organization with the capacity to continue our mission.

Reflecting on my experience, I see that the center's friction and challenges were often related to waning relationships. Therapists felt the board was out of touch with the pandemic-driven realities they faced. Donors felt lost and unappreciated in the leadership churn. The board felt frustrated by the need for more information and transparency.

This chapter introduces two relational approaches I illustrate throughout the book:

1. The competing values framework
2. My leadership model

COMPETING VALUES FRAMEWORK

My exposure to the competing values framework (CVF) has changed how I approach leadership, communication, and strategic planning. The CVF is depicted as two continuums: internal versus external and flexible versus rigid. Most organizational friction arises when values are misaligned or at least perceived as misaligned.

Imagine a board of directors meeting at a publicly traded company where constituents discuss the organization's strategic plan. On the one hand, you have an aggressive timeline and pressure to drive growth to satisfy investors. On the other side lies the need for systematic strategic planning, resource-consuming talent optimization, and arduous culture building. Trying to satisfy both creates friction, but both sides believe their strategy is in the organization's best interests.

The above example illustrates how competing values play out at the macro level, but value friction also occurs in our daily routines and the spontaneous choices we make. A parable tells of two people walking by a stream when they notice babies floating down the river. The short version is: One starts grabbing the babies out of the river while the other begins to run upstream. The first asks, "Where are you going? We have to save these babies!" The second replies, "I'm going to see who's throwing babies in the river."

The first individual focused on the crisis (internal); the second focused on a solution beyond the obvious (external).

Often, we find ourselves entrenched in a position without understanding the other side's perspective or the values that inform it. Consider no-kill animal shelters. People on both sides of the debate are equally passionate and committed. The discussion often concerns a conflict of values between saving life and quality of life. Are resources better utilized to address the root cause of the problem by promoting spaying and neutering pets and feral animals or using precious resources for shelter animals who may be unadoptable?

I'm not arguing that one approach is right or morally superior. I'm suggesting that the CVF can be a tool for creating shared understanding and values alignment. You may disagree with another's values, but understanding their perspective is valuable for tying decisions to an organization's purpose and mission.

The CVF is valuable for more than communication and conflict resolution. When considering a group's collective values, it can help:

- Determine a team's strengths and gaps.
- Identify effective learning approaches.
- Inform career planning, individual or team development, and talent recruitment.
- Map leadership roles and responsibilities.
- Design a new organization or department.

Consider my nonprofit's board of directors. Understanding each board member's values would help with committee assignments, finding ways to leverage their strengths, and engaging them in meaningful work. The knowledge would also help the board have a rigorous debate to pursue the best strategic plan.

Faith-based groups founded the nonprofit. For some board members, that legacy was critical; for others, it was irrelevant. Some board members were passionate about keeping the entity; others were passionate about maintaining the mission. Like many boards, we had doers, talkers, and nodders—people who went along to get along. Some people wanted to roll up their sleeves and contribute while others appreciated it when work got done but opted for the path of least resistance.

The point is our values influence our actions and behaviors. Misconceptions like those created by capitalists and altruists are everywhere. Understanding the other's values is often the solution to eliminating friction, building engagement, and fostering psychological safety.

LEADERSHIP MODEL

Since leaders are the standard bearers for work culture, my bias for how to approach leadership comes from the Schein camp, which I shared in the introduction to this book: "because culture constrains strategy, a company must analyze its culture and learn to manage within its boundaries or, if necessary, change it."[2] Therefore, I envision leadership as a four-step process:

1. **Leading Yourself**—As a leader, you must recognize your biases, motivations, and values. You must have the strategic awareness to understand and recognize how people will make sense of your behaviors—intentional or unintentional.
2. **Leading Others**—Leaders must own their shadow. In the trickle-down reality of life inside organizations, a leader's words and deeds disproportionately affect how people structure the unknown, frame their experiences, and go about their day.

Leaders can influence the sensemaking narrative by being consistent, emotionally intelligent, and building relationships. When you are just and fair, employees deem you trustworthy. When employees trust you, they give you the benefit of the doubt when you fail. As you develop meaningful relationships, employees believe you will extend them the same benefit of the doubt. Sensing the environment is psychologically safe frees them to be vulnerable and take risks.

3. **Engineering Culture**—A leader's role should include repeatedly communicating the why. This

connection to purpose helps align values and elevates commitment to the tasks.[3] Consider how employees perceive support and the role your behavior plays. Ask yourself:

- o Have you communicated company goals, aspirations, and values so employees understand the mission?
- o Do they have cognitive structural clarity about how the mission gets accomplished and their role?
- o Do your people feel a sense of acceptance, inclusion, and belonging that allows them to engage fully?
- o Do employees have the necessary resources and feel supported in pursuing shared goals?
- o Is the environment an accountable and safe learning culture that encourages risk-taking so that an individual's need for self-preservation does not trump the organization's objectives?

You cannot let culture happen. Leaders must make culture happen. Aspirations set the tone for your culture, but it is defined by what leaders tolerate from themselves and others. Your behaviors and words must align with your stated values and mission.

4. **Executing Strategy**—In theory, you could define strategy at any point. However, understanding how your culture's boundaries are rate-limiting can prevent work from being done in vain. Additionally, through building relationships, you will better understand the capacity and potential of your resources. This knowledge will allow you to optimize your human

capital and align it with your mission. Only then does executing strategy make sense.

THE EASY WAY OR THE HARD WAY?

I was venting to my wife about our five-year-old daughter being a "tiny dictator." She exasperated me because everything was a battle. I had resorted to saying, "We can do this the easy way or the hard way." My daughter almost always opted for the hard way. For example, it took three people to administer eye drops when she had pink eye. My wife said, "She is stubborn, just like you."

It made me think of my paternal grandfather. His name was Myrle. As a child, he must have had a lot in common with my stubborn daughter because one of his siblings nicknamed him Ted—after the family mule. (I'm sure many people will find it fitting that my namesake is a jackass.)

I was curious if the legend of stubborn mules was true. When I Googled "Mule won't cooperate," the first hit was the Pushy Mule discussion board. In the thread, someone wrote, "You can generally 'make' or 'intimidate' a horse into cooperating with you, but that won't work with a mule. The mule has to see the advantage of partnering with you, and it will take some time to show him that you are worthy."

Too often, I have resorted to a *we can do this the easy way or the hard way* management approach because I did not have the patience to build relationships. I've learned leadership can be like parenting and, evidently, working with mules. The success generated the hard way may be fast, but it is fleeting.

It is an investment to build relationships and to understand and align your employees' values, but the payoff can be a work culture that supports your strategy rather than constraining it.

KEY CHAPTER TAKEAWAYS

- A direct relationship exists between engagement and an employee's relationship with their manager.
- Most organizational friction arises when values are misaligned or at least perceived as misaligned.
- Understanding the other's values is often the solution to eliminating friction, building engagement, and fostering psychological safety.
- Aspirations set the tone for your culture, but what a leader tolerates from themselves and others defines culture.

CHAPTER 2:

PARADIGM SHIFT

"The purpose of learning isn't to affirm our beliefs; it's to evolve our beliefs."

—ADAM GRANT

Why do I believe psychological safety is paramount to organizational success? The hook for me was listening to Dr. Edmonson describe a research quandary when she spoke at the orientation weekend of my Doctoral program. While researching high-performing nursing teams, Edmondson's data suggested that nurses making the most mistakes had the best patient outcomes.

That seemed contradictory.

However, it made perfect sense when she realized they were not making more mistakes. The high-performing teams' errors were seeing the light of day. They experienced a psychologically safe environment where the benefits of speaking up—improved patient care, learning collaboration, quality control, and error prevention—outweighed the potential consequences of making a mistake. Meanwhile, the poor performers were not making fewer errors. They were just less likely to report them.

What I've come to understand is psychological safety isn't a solution. It's a result. It emerges from a shared history of collaborating, failing, and winning to achieve common goals. It materializes when people feel supported by their peers, leaders, and organizations. This realization started my evolution from a directive "do it because I said so" boss to embracing relationships and cultivating psychological safety as a better model for leadership.

IT IS OUR WORLD; THEY ARE JUST WALKING THROUGH IT.

My first management job was at UPS when I was twenty years old. I started as a part-time package handler and eventually worked my way into a frontline supervisor role. My boss, Joe, was an easygoing, benevolent man, an uncommon trait in an often-contentious union environment. I remember getting quality control reports from Joe with stars and red smiley faces like a schoolteacher would draw. I never heard him raise his voice. Even our Teamsters Union steward genuinely seemed to like him. People trusted him. He passed out well wishes and handshakes like Oprah Winfrey did giveaways—one for you, one for you, one for you.

Then, abruptly, he was transferred to another center.

His successor, Craig, drove a shiny black BMW coupe. He wore dapper tailored suits, slicked-back silver fox hair, and a pencil-thin mustache. Craig could have been a mob boss out of central casting. He had been a manager from another regional center, and his battle-tested reputation preceded him. He did not shy away from conflict and was direct with his communication.

Our management team quickly learned his motto: "It is our world. They (the unionized staff) are just walking through it."

I don't think our center's workforce ever felt psychologically safe under either leader, but the trust my first boss nurtured quickly dissolved. There is inherent conflict in a union environment, and the us versus them mindset is a barrier to feeling psychologically safe. The union employees' sense of safety came from their representation, but it did not mean they sensed the environment was safe for risk-taking. Big Brother was always watching.

Despite the inherent tension, my first boss, Joe, still communicated that he cared about his people. Employees quickly learned that with Craig, business came first.

Imagine you are a driver whose average workday is ten hours long, and your daughter has preschool graduation at five o'clock. Contractually, you could request a certain number of eight-hour days for these circumstances. If you had exhausted your eight-hour requests or management had granted more senior drivers the day's allotment, you might still strike a bargain with Joe. With Craig, you had better hustle if you wanted to see more than a picture of her in a cap and gown.

As we will discuss throughout this book, context matters. Whether it was Craig's leadership philosophy or how he managed because a collectively bargained contract arbitrated outcomes, two contrasting leadership styles were at play— one for the leadership team and another for union employees. While the unionized workforce's morale was in decline, the leadership team saw a different side of Craig. He loved to laugh and joke and was a great mentor.

The reason for Craig's Jekyll and Hyde persona did not matter. As the union employees made sense of his behavior, they felt victimized. Research has found that when employees feel treated unjustly, they often try to correct the relational balance by withholding discretionary effort, doing the bare minimum required,[1] or even engaging in acts counter to norms or expected behaviors.[2] Friction intensified.

EATING CROW

Several months after Craig arrived, I decided I was a vital cog and leveraged that assumption to get a raise. I walked into Craig's office and explained that I had another job offer and needed more money if he wanted me to stay. He turned solemn and then suggested I go home and do an experiment.

His instructions were to fill my bathtub with about four inches of water. He was insistent that the level be just right. He revisited the proper depth several times and then moved on to the water temperature. It, too, had to be just right—like a hot tub—104 degrees. Then I was to place my index finger in the water, but only up to the second knuckle. I was to swirl it around three times. After the water settles, I should pull my finger out quickly.

"See how long it takes the hole to fill in," he said. "That is how long it will take me to replace you."

He burst past me out of his office—trying hard but failing to contain his laughter—hopped in his BMW and sped off. While it may seem cruel, it was what I needed. I was a cocky kid. He was skilled at building relationships, understanding his audience, and tailoring lessons to make his point.

The next day, I crawled into his office with my tail between my legs. Within minutes, we were howling about my terrible poker face. This approach could have been risky, but he knew me as a person and trusted in the relationship he had fostered. The ruse became a story that connected us.

I tested our relationship again a few months later. I was responsible for ensuring all outbound packages got off the trucks and routed to their destinations. The most critical piece of the job was getting the guaranteed Next Day Air packages processed to make connections at the airport. At the time, overnight delivery was a new service, and this product line was UPS's highest priority. I performed a quality check on each truck to verify it was empty. About 10 p.m. one night, long after the connection at the airport had departed, a hysterical employee brought me twenty-three Next Day Air letters that I had missed.

I knew I was fired. As I began sorting through the envelopes, I noticed only a few local deliveries, but several more were in-state. Illinois parcels went to a hub that was only two hours away. If I was lucky, I could make the connection, and the parcels headed for Chicago would avoid becoming service failures. I raced toward the hub, but I didn't make it. I told the manager I would drive the remaining packages to Chicago. It was only another three hours. Could he please give me directions? I still remember his befuddled look. He said flatly, "Just go home, kid."

I got home about 3 a.m. There was no sleeping. I knew Craig got to the distribution center around 6 a.m. I was there waiting for him when he arrived. Again, I crawled into his office with my tail between my legs—this time to offer my resignation. He had no idea what I was talking about. I could sense his anger rising as it became clear what had happened and the recognition that he would pay for my mistake. My failure was a direct reflection on him.

Then he did something I didn't expect. He thanked me for my extra efforts to mitigate service failures, told me I was too hard on myself, built me back up, and told me how important I was to his team.

The last thing he said was not a surprise. "If you ever do that again, I will fire you on the spot."

PSYCHOLOGICAL SAFETY

As a mid-level manager, I have reported to many people. I've watched leaders use different styles and have seen how those behaviors affect morale and work cultures. I have also reflected on how their behaviors affected me.

With my first UPS boss, Joe, I had a sense of security based more on contentment and harmony. I did my job. Looking back, Craig pushed me beyond my comfort zone, and I voluntarily contributed more than my job description required. I knew he had my back, so I took risks and learned from failures—big and small. I trusted Joe. I felt psychologically safe with Craig.

These experiences from my past illustrate some essential traits of psychological safety and what I ultimately researched—how leader behaviors foster or hinder psychologically safe work cultures. Research on psychological safety analyzes the construct at three levels: individual, team, and organizational.[3] Psychological safety occurs when one individual decides to be vulnerable by contributing when they could simply eliminate any risk by remaining silent.

In an organizational context, a single act of courage is like throwing an ice cube into a warm swimming pool. However, psychological safety can aggregate if vulnerable behaviors are modeled, encouraged, and rewarded. Constructive conflict can emerge as the need for self-protection fades within a group, resulting in better decisions and outcomes.

Psychological safety is not the absence of disagreement but the group's ability to productively deal with differences to safely problem solve, innovate, and succeed. The team may not achieve consensus but can gain a shared understanding, allowing people to disagree but move forward.

KEY CHAPTER TAKEAWAYS

1. Feeling psychologically safe creates a learning environment where failure is an opportunity for growth, not a punitive event.
2. Employees develop psychological safety by making sense of environmental cues, the most influential of which is a leader's behavior.
3. An individual experiences psychological safety, but when it aggregates as a team-level trait, its benefits are realized, allowing for constructive conflict.

CHAPTER 3:

LEADERS ARE
ALWAYS ON STAGE

"It's not what you look at that matters; it's what you see."

—HENRY DAVID THOREAU

On June 7, 1893, bigots forcibly removed a young lawyer from a whites-only train car in South Africa. His prejudiced expulsion launched Mohandas Karamchand Gandhi, later known as "The Mahatma" (Great-Souled), on a passive resistance crusade that influenced civil rights movements worldwide.[1]

Martin Luther King Jr. rose to prominence as the leader of the United States Civil Rights Movement from 1954 until his assassination in 1968. King credited Gandhi's behaviors of showing love and modeling nonviolence as "the method for social reform that I had been seeking."[2]

In 1964, Nelson Mandela, another lawyer and advocate of nonviolent resistance, began serving an unjust twenty-seven-year prison sentence in his quest to end apartheid in South Africa. After the end of apartheid, he became the first democratically elected president of South Africa. He devoted his life to spreading the same philosophy of nonviolence in pursuing freedom and equality in other countries.

These three mavericks of peace who achieved significant political and social progress inspired countless people by modeling behavior. They accomplished revolution through passive resistance despite tremendous social and political pressure to revert to violence. They moved masses by demonstrating desired behaviors, often at great personal sacrifice.

Leaders are always on stage. Their role sets an organizational tone down the chain of command through their actions, words, and deeds. Employees' perceptions evolve based on sensemaking as they scrutinize interactions, observe peers, and scan the environment for clues about organizational norms and values.

Imagine being a young Civil Rights activist and witnessing Dr. King's total commitment to nonviolence despite knowing his methods were unpopular and his life was in danger. He was arrested twenty-nine times for acts of civil disobedience,[3] and he was assaulted at least four times.[4] King paid the ultimate price for his cause on April 4, 1968. He was assassinated while standing on a balcony of his second-floor room at the Lorraine Motel in Memphis, Tennessee.

Dr. King inspired generations of civil rights leaders, and we have a national holiday to celebrate his legacy and commitment to living out his values. A leader's behavior does not need to be Nobel Prize-worthy to affect others. Routine behaviors influence employees' sensemaking.

What behaviors are your employees making sense of?

- If you pass by litter when entering the building, do you pick it up?
- If your team works late or comes in on weekends, do you join them?
- If you preach about diversity and inclusion, does the demographic makeup of your senior team reflect that value?
- Do you give employees personal time off yet send emails and take meetings while on vacation?
- Does your organization espouse the values of quality and safety, yet your key performance metrics are all financial?

Employees constantly make sense of behaviors like these and look for gaps between what leaders say and how they act.

BODY LANGUAGE IS NEVER SILENT

What happens when you meet someone new? Research shows that we begin to form an impression of a stranger within seconds.[5] Changing others' opinions of you after developing a first impression is difficult because they will view your actions through that lens.[6]

How people make sense of your body language helps determine if they perceive you as trustworthy. When introduced, a new acquaintance subliminally evaluates your facial expressions, eye contact, and posture. Social psychologists call this process of making snap judgments with minimal information "thin-slicing."[7] This prejudging is a relic of our evolution, a holdover from when making instant decisions about friend or foe was critical to survival.

It is daunting to consider a first interaction with someone a make-or-break moment. Luckily, while that initial impression is sticky, it is malleable. Dr. Ron Riggio explains that the research around first impressions might be overblown in a work context. He describes how our initial impressions are important, but the process is cumulative. "I think as you learn more information, you start to revise that schema you have of the person."

Riggio, the Henry R. Kravis professor of leadership and organizational psychology at Claremont McKenna College, said there is an incentive to cooperate in work settings. Many of these "snap judgment" studies happen in a laboratory vacuum. In an interview, he told me, "I think you can do a 180 degree regarding your initial impression of people if you have an opportunity to interact... We are constantly processing, so the only way I think first impressions really matter is if the person decides I've got no reason to deal with this person further."

When sensemaking, people simultaneously interpret messages from two channels. Consciously and subconsciously, employees are evaluating verbal and nonverbal communication.

Employees read between the lines to decide if the messages are congruent and trustworthy.

Leaders may spend months crafting a perfect strategic plan, but when it is delivered, physical cues matter, too. Body language, facial expressions, mannerisms, and other unintended actions might sabotage communication. Put simply, if the messages in the communication channels don't match, the leader does not make sense.

In the 1970s, Albert Mehrabian of the University of California in Los Angeles studied emotional communication. His research showed the communication content is much less critical than the delivery. Only 7 percent of communication was attributable to the words. Body language accounted for 55 percent of the communication, and tone accounted for 38 percent.[8] Leader behavior consultant Carol Kinsey Goman explains, "Volume, pitch, inflection, pace, rhythm, rate, intensity, clarity, pauses—all of these play a role in *how* you say what you say—and that 'how' can sometimes be more revealing of your true intent than the 'what' contained in the words."[9]

Think about the statement, "That's nice." You could use it in response to someone reminiscing about a lost loved one, a dude falling while executing a gnarly skateboard move, or being shown a diamond engagement ring. Context matters whether "that's nice" is empathetic, sarcastic, or enthusiastic.

Nonverbal behaviors encompass a wide range of signals that can significantly affect communication. For example, savvy leaders understand something as simple as a smile can communicate, "I'm approachable. I don't bite." These cues often convey more information than words and impact a message's meaning. These word-free messages can play a crucial role in establishing trust and credibility.

When our communication partners do not share our language or cultural backgrounds, nonverbal communication plays a salient role, allowing us to communicate volumes without the benefit of a shared language.[10] Facial expressions can communicate happiness, surprise, anger, confusion, or other feelings. Eye contact signals engagement, interest, and attentiveness. Hand movements, posture, and proximity can enhance communication, show confidence, and convey caring or formality.

Each culture can uniquely interpret nonverbal behaviors. For example, in Indian, African, and Middle Eastern cultures, people always use their right hand for formal tasks like greeting, touching, and eating.[11] They use their left hand to tidy up after going to the bathroom and consider it unclean.[12]

Your audience is keen on subtle involuntary facial expressions and nervous habits that can reveal a person's genuine emotions, even when you are intentionally trying to hide them. They subconsciously watch for cues communicating whether you understand cultural norms and individual preferences. For example, maintaining eye contact is another nonverbal behavior that can vary dramatically based on the culture.

In Western cultures, eye contact can enhance communication, be viewed as a sign of respect, and project self-confidence. However, in some Asian cultures, too much eye contact is viewed as disrespectful.[13] Japanese children are taught to look at adults' necks when communicating to maintain peripheral visibility without being impolite.[14] Being mindful of these norms can help avoid misunderstandings or offending others and is crucial for successful communication.

I've noticed that when my nonverbal cues do not align with my message, they create doubt. People misunderstand my reserved nature as aloofness. My lack of expressiveness and emotion have made me seem unapproachable and even callous.

As a leader, I must be strategically aware of the unintended signals I'm sending. I must focus on active listening by maintaining eye contact, nodding in acknowledgment, and using appropriate facial expressions to show I'm engaged and attentive. I must also consistently make a conscious effort to interact with people because my default setting is to sidestep socializing. I have learned that simple acts like smiling, patting someone on the back, or giving a thumbs-up can convey approval and boost morale.

AN OPEN INVITATION
Leaders have an inherent disadvantage when communicating because of the perception positional power may create in an employee's mind. The innate

distrust of authority and a leader's ability to administer rewards and punishments can inhibit communication[15] because employees are likely only to speak up when the benefits outweigh the risks.[16]

A leader's perceived approachability is vital to a subordinate feeling safe to speak up,[17] as is the leader taking time to consider ideas and employees believing the leader will act.[18] Edmondson recommends three leader behaviors that enhance psychological safety and invite participation:

- Accessibility means a leader is approachable and available. A leader may have an open-door policy, but do employees feel heard after dropping in?
- Inviting input involves seeking others' opinions and being open to discussion. Do leaders consider the devil's advocate perspectives when making decisions, or are their minds made up, and soliciting feedback is just a formality?
- Modeling openness and fallibility involves owning mistakes and setting an example. Even outstanding leaders can make deeply flawed decisions. Should these mistakes be buried to avoid embarrassment, or can leaders share their learnings and admit their fallibility?[19]

Nembhard and Edmondson labeled these three leader behaviors "inclusive leadership," which they define as "words and deeds by a leader or leaders that indicate an invitation and appreciation for others' contributions."[20]

BEST FRIENDS FOREVER

Is there a point of diminishing returns on inclusivity and relational leadership? That question illustrates an uncomfortable reality for many new leaders after a promotion. The elephant in the room is, "Can I still be friends with my direct reports?"

During our interview, I posed that question to Dr. Riggio. Our discussion shifted to the academic research on leadership. He pointed out how transformational leadership represents this paradox. "In the transformational leadership model, that's the idealized influence. You want to look like a leader, but then the other side is the individualized consideration. You also want to develop a relationship, but you still have to maintain that leadership gravitas," he said.

To be effective, leaders must build relationships with their employees. Whether they can be friends hinges on the maturity of the relationship and the individuals. When things go wrong, and they inevitably will, both parties must be able to separate the undesirable conduct from the desirable individual who displayed the behavior. Can you be friends with your employees? As with most things in leadership, it depends on the context.

FOSTERING PSYCHOLOGICAL SAFETY. WHAT IS A LEADER TO DO?

Psychological safety is closely related to the construct of trust. However, two subtle differences make it unique. First, trust focuses on giving someone else the benefit of the doubt (e.g., when a mistake occurs) while psychological safety is about whether you believe the other will provide you the benefit of the doubt. Second, trust relates to the anticipated consequence of an event that may linger into the future while psychological safety focuses on the outcome of a specific action.[21]

A study attempting to describe preferred leader prototypes shows the challenge of defining what leader behaviors foster psychological safety. There was no consensus among people on what makes a good leader: 38 percent of participants endorsed a prototypical ideal leader, 30 percent supported a laissez-faire ideal leader (disengaged, passive), 19 percent endorsed an ideal leader who is autocratic (narcissistic, pushy), and 14 percent endorsed an anti-prototypical leader (tyrannical).[22] This study's findings of preferred leader behaviors illustrate the challenge of knowing how to act.

Dr. Riggio emphasized this contextual challenge of leadership. "Too much of the popular literature; it's like a recipe. Follow the recipe, and you'll get these outcomes, but it is much more subtle than that," he told me. "I've done work on impression management, and we know how people can make more positive impressions, but the other side of this is authenticity. You want to influence people, or you want to have a certain impact on them, but also being yourself is important. It's a really delicate balance."

Often, leaders are on stage and do not know it. Imagine, heading to the breakroom, you walk past an office and overhear a manager chastising someone about saying *um, ah,* and *like* during a presentation. Based on similar feedback you previously received from a boss you disliked, you make sense of the feedback as critical. Maybe you missed the explanation that an audience can interpret filler words as hesitant or make the speaker seem lacking in knowledge or sophistication. In context, the supervisor or employee may experience the discussion as constructive.

What if you recount what you witnessed to two colleagues when you got to the breakroom? The downstream effect of this is people can frame their experience through someone else's lens. The rumor mill can create a vicarious acquisition of fears.[23] A leader's "reputation" may precede them, regardless of whether the reputation is warranted. This assumption can create a scenario where an employee is afraid of a leader despite never having a bad experience with them.[24] These scenarios emphasize how leaders are always on stage and knowing how to act is ambiguous. Strong relationships built on trust can buffer a leader's reputation.

INFORMAL LEADERSHIP
In 1993, outspoken NBA basketball star Charles Barkley appeared in a Nike commercial, proclaiming, "I am not a role model."[25]

Barkley used his notoriety and platform to make a point. As he spoke in schools, he noticed a disparity between the aspirations of white and black students. "When I was going to these schools, I said, well, how many of y'all want to play sports, and I noticed at the black schools, pretty much every kid raised their hand," Barkley said in an interview on the basketball Network website.[26] "But when I go to a white school, I said well, how many of y'all want to play sports, only about 10 percent raised their hand. We got too many black kids that think they can only be successful through athletics and entertainment; they don't think they can be doctors and lawyers and engineers and shit like that."

The commercial started a heated debate about role models and whether kids should emulate their parents rather than athletes or celebrities. Barkley described the commercial as "probably the most important thing I've done."[27] His genius was understanding that formal and informal leaders are held in high regard, whether they want to be or not. He used his platform to lead a meaningful conversation by creating a controversy.

Regardless of your title, how will you use your stage to lead when there is no avoiding the spotlight?

KEY CHAPTER TAKEAWAYS
- Leaders hold the key to setting an organizational tone down the chain of command through their actions, words, and deeds.
- Nonverbal behaviors are also critical inputs in the employee sensemaking process.
- Psychological safety is closely related to trust. However, trust focuses on giving someone else the

benefit of the doubt (e.g., when an employee makes a mistake) while psychological safety is about whether you believe the other will extend you that same courtesy. Second, trust relates to the anticipated consequence of an event that may linger into the future while psychological safety focuses on the outcome of a specific action in the moment.

CHAPTER 4:

THE MAN IN THE MIRROR

"Not until we are lost do we begin to understand ourselves."

—ATTRIBUTED TO HENRY DAVID THOREAU

In high school, I got into an altercation with my sophomore baseball coach, and we exchanged cutting insults and nearly blows. Afterward, I feared the coach would kick me off the team. My dad took me to meet a family friend for advice. After I described my predicament, the friend told me, "When you get to be my age, and someone calls you a jerk, it is okay because you know it is true."

The discussion was more expansive, but that sentiment helped set me on a different path. I credit that conversation from thirty-five years ago with making it okay to be my introverted self and not have to please everyone. This notion has provided a foundation for making unpopular decisions as a leader. The advice gave me the courage to stand with the minority, or even alone, for what I believe. This chapter reflects on the first step of my leadership model from chapter 1—leading yourself.

We are all products of our environment. I grew up in Edwardsville, Illinois. In the 1970s–80s, it was still a small rural community. My exposure to diversity (people, cultures, and thoughts) was narrow and remained so for much of my adult life. In 2017, I enrolled in a PhD program at Benedictine University's Center for Values-Driven Leadership.

The experience stretched me in ways I did not fathom were possible. The academic literature expanded my understanding of what it means to lead. The results of dozens of behavioral and leadership assessments forced me to come to terms with some unpleasant truths about my personality, behaviors, and leadership. It was an opportunity to reflect on issues I had never considered. My classmates helped lead me down a path of personal growth.

One of our first assignments was to write a blog post about our understanding of leadership for the center's website. *Employees—Treat Them Like Dogs?* was the title of my blog. Somewhat in jest, I contrasted my management experience, such as my belief that accountability and consistency were critical, with how Cesar Milan, the celebrity "Dog Whisperer," approached training dogs. I concluded the assignment like this:

"The key to leading people is not being a one-trick pony. Effective leadership requires having a depth of skills to manage each challenge uniquely. I would never suggest publicizing, 'We treat our employees like dogs.' It could hamper recruitment efforts. However, I can make the case for treating employees like dogs in the context that expectations are clear, and leadership is consistent. Feedback, good and bad, is immediate and not a once-a-year attack at review time. Managers show employees appreciation (positive reinforcement). The appropriate leadership style is used, each in the right measure, at just the right time. Sometimes, employees need a treat, verbal encouragement, or a pat on the back; other times, they need a 'tsch!' or firm tap."

I felt like I had written a solid blog. Despite its whimsical nature, I thought it captured what I knew to be true about leadership—a lack of accountability was the root cause of most problems. In hindsight, the assignment's feedback was the first indication I was an outlier in the program. Most people who self-select into a values-driven leadership program are not directive leaders. A chasm existed between what I knew about leadership and what I was about to learn.

"Ted, I appreciate your blog. Your writing is strong and your topic an important one, but I'm not sure I am comfortable publishing it on the CVDL blog in its current form," the program's director wrote at the bottom of my paper. "I feel like it is unnecessarily harsh to say things like treat employees like dogs, even though I know what you mean, and it comes with a question mark. I am also not comfortable with promoting coercive leadership, finger jabs, and pinch collars, even though again, when read in detail and in context, I get what you are trying to say. All that said, I think the topic of having the courage to have candor and provide constructive feedback, even to the point of letting people go, is an important one... both as a way to improve individual and organizational performance and as a way to do what is best for the employee him or herself. I hope you will consider revising the blog with an eye to publishing it....The blog is still well-written and thoughtful and addresses an important topic from a values-driven perspective."

In hindsight, I was not considering the undertones of a white man invoking a metaphor to treat employees like animals. This feedback was one of many occasions when I discovered how my naiveté, ignorance, and lack of emotional intelligence were detrimental to my leadership.

I frequently had the experience of square peg pounded into a round hole. For example, I remember balking at the idea that leaders could accomplish everything through kindness because people are inherently wired for good. I quickly conjured up a list of former employees whose redeeming qualities had never been identified.

That weekend, I was assigned a study about people's "innate moral core." Researchers showed preverbal babies a puppet show where one puppet was mean to the other. When offered the puppets, babies consistently selected the nice puppet over the mean one.[1] Conceptually, I always understood that most people were inherently good, but it had never been a conscious part of my leadership calculus. Each revelation like this, and there were many, chipped away at what I thought I knew about leadership, relationships, and people in general.

WHO ARE WE?

Early in our program, before I knew my peers, we had a small-group development course that spanned two weekends. The course began with an abstract discussion of authenticity: What is it? Where does it reside? Is it real? The discussion irked me because I consider myself an authentic person. I take pride in being genuine. It seemed like heresy to question the legitimacy of authentic people. Of course, I know myself and present the real me in every encounter, or so I thought.

As part of the course, we completed the Johari Window exercise, which helps people better understand their relationships with themselves and others. I fell into a category labeled the turtle. "This type of person tends to be the silent member or 'observer,' neither giving nor soliciting feedback."[2] I doubt that many people aspire to turtledom, but I found something familiar and comforting in that description.

I was proud to be a turtle until I read the description's conclusion. "...such persons learn very little about themselves because they do not provide the group with any data to which it can react...Energy channeled in maintaining a closed system is not available for self-exploration and personal growth."[3]

I was living in a vacuum.

THE EXPERIMENT

Early the first weekend, our instructors divided us into two teams and sent us to separate rooms. We sat there with minimal direction for four agonizing hours, often in silence. If you're wondering what we were supposed to do in those rooms, don't worry. So were we.

While everyone experienced anxiety and annoyance at the outset, circumstances exacerbated my frustration. My dad had passed away the previous week. I struggled with surrendering to the process and being a guinea pig. After the first four hours, we broke for lunch. Then the instructor introduced an exercise to nudge us through the group evolution experience. The activity was intended to make us vulnerable.

The instructor asked us to introduce ourselves from the perspective of someone who knew our shortcomings. The introductions became more intense and personal as we went around the circle. Every time I considered an introduction, my thoughts drifted to Dad. I was unwilling to give that much of myself. I left the room just as my dam broke.

As I regained my composure in the lounge, my thoughts kept returning to the morning's discussion of authenticity. Why is it so hard for me to interact socially or engage strangers? Do I really prefer isolation? Three months earlier, at our program's opening weekend, where Dr. Edmondson was the keynote speaker, I had spent the networking time lurking in the stairwell or hiding in the bathroom rather than leveraging the golden opportunity to meet people who could help me on my professional journey. Nothing about that was authentic.

In another exercise, a Black woman, whom I'll refer to as Wall Street, explained a day in her life. I was dismayed.

It was troubling to learn that people must scan the room and scrutinize every action or comment to fit their audience. The description of all the different "masks" or personas Wall Street wore to "be accepted" as a Black woman in our culture sounded exhausting.

I understood the challenge of trust in groups from a new perspective. I also began to understand privilege, inclusion, and the challenges marginalized people face in ways I had never considered. Can leaders cultivate openness to these topics without an experience like this? Furthermore, can psychological safety be created without an internalized understanding of the elements that drive its development?

At the end of the immersive group development experiment, our peers provided feedback about how they experienced us. When Wall Street received her feedback, some suggested that she was too direct and that her communication would benefit from less candor. She had heard the message before: "Quit being the angry black woman."

I paid forward my mentor's reliable counsel about it being okay to be a jerk. "You can't own others' feelings or their perceptions of you," I told her. Another woman of color in my group, an HR executive, patiently waited until everyone else had spoken. Then she implored Wall Street—while educating the rest of us—to be her "authentic self" because, as a Black woman, she risked being "pushed aside" in the professional world if she failed to advocate for herself vehemently.

I recently revisited this experience with Wall Street. Given her career in the financial sector, she said the HR executive's advice was spot on. "I have to establish my place among these white men in certain cases, so they don't just automatically think that I'm there to get coffee." She has been hearing similar feedback her entire life, and terms like "constructive contentiousness" have littered her performance appraisals.

"Remember my Johari Window?" Wall Street said. "It is to share who I am authentically....Clearly, I am not a turtle." That seemed like a contradiction because of all the masks she described wearing. My education continued as she explained those masks were not for her. "I'm always covering something to make others feel comfortable with me." It was how she struck a balance between retaining her identity and conforming to a group.

JAM SESSION

Not long after the group experiment, Wall Street, the HR executive, and two other Black classmates invited me to join them in the lobby of a Hampton Inn to decompress after a long day. As the evening wore on, a Name-That-Tuneish jam session replaced the academic banter. Someone would call up a song on their phone, and often, before it got to the chorus, another person would change the station by launching one of their playlist favorites into the evening. For hours, an eclectic mix of R&B, rock and roll, hip-hop, and pop flowed—as did the drink.

"Remember this one?"

"I got one for you."

And on it went. Laughter and a sporadic sharing of bygone events punctuated the patchwork recital. Despite, again, feeling like a square peg in a round hole, the unique experience with new friends was liberating. Then someone cautioned that it was getting late, and we were being too loud. Another said, "It's all right. We got our token Whitey here. They won't say a word to us." It may have been the first time in my life when being in the out-group was so evident.

These jam sessions became a ritual I never missed. We had deep, challenging conversations about understanding each other and developing shared meaning. Not only did I gain an appreciation for Motown, but I also gained the opportunity to experience "the other." The sessions were real-life small group development. I got as much education in the Hampton Inn lobby as in the classroom.

WHO AM I?
Like Wall Street, we each received feedback. When it was my turn, Wall Street said she recognized my desire for personal space and tried to respect it. Others were not as gentle. I was labeled a "self-negated extrovert." The group suggested I was hiding behind a phony introvert's shield.

I began questioning the authenticity and stoic façade I was so proud of. What I was considering is: Who am I? Is my idea of authentic self just a self-limiting mask? Is my independent persona nothing more than a giant defense mechanism? Is my highly polished shell just a manifestation of the belief that if others truly knew me, they would undoubtedly reject me? How did I get into this shell if I am not a turtle? More importantly, if I decide to, how can I get out?

As I reflected on past experiences—times of vulnerability or of being misunderstood—I realized I was not just robbing myself of opportunity; I was harming others.

I recalled being dumbstricken by a boss promoting me to a manager role "despite your arrogance." In hindsight, I was suffering from imposter syndrome, and my default defense mechanism to withdrawal had kicked in. My boss perceived my behavior as brash and standoffish, which was the opposite of my reality. My interpretation of my early lesson about individualism changed. Always retreating to my shell made me appear self-absorbed. I wasn't just comfortable being labeled a jerk; that was how people were experiencing me.

COME TOGETHER

In 2014, I began working in my father's veterinary hospital. A young woman I was mentoring was a victim of a domestic violence attack. She had recently joined our leadership team, so I arranged to hold the next management meeting at her parents' home, where she was staying. We brought the family a catered meal.

The meeting had a minimal agenda. I had talked with Dad and his business partner beforehand, and they pledged to help her in any way the corporation could. When I tried to express that over lunch, I got choked up. Surrounded by total strangers, five of whom were new direct reports, I could not get the words out. Some of it was anger at her attacker, and some of it was watching her hold her toddler, still looking terrified. Part of it was my pride in our company's commitment to employees.

That event forged a connection with the team that otherwise may have never happened. I was no longer the aloof, indifferent new boss. I was suddenly a caring human being. My authentic, albeit embarrassing, response allowed that small group to view me differently.

Patrick Lencioni is a best-selling author who writes about team dynamics. He says, "Teamwork begins by building trust. And the only way to do that is to overcome our need for invulnerability."[4]

REPUTATION AND IDENTITY

Hogan is an assessment company specializing in personality, which it describes as "a person's disposition or core wiring and the thoughts, feelings, and behaviors that stem from it." Hogan bifurcates personality into two perspectives. "We are experts on our personalities from an inside view, which can be defined as *identity*....Others do not have access to the Pollyannaish stories of our identities. Instead, they experience our personalities from an outside view to decide the other major component of our personalities: reputation."[5]

Put simply, identity is how we view ourselves; reputation is how others view us. Your reputation—how others perceive you—determines whether the boss hires you, the results of your performance reviews, and your opportunities for advancement. People make and act on decisions about you all day, every day, and those choices are based on your reputation, not on your identity. Whether employees follow you is determined by your reputation. All consequential decisions are based on who others think you are, not who you believe you are.

Knowing yourself will help you be strategically self-aware and regulate the signals others use to make sense of you and their work environment. Too often, leaders are fixated on their identity when they need to understand their reputation because of the considerable role it plays in others' sensemaking experience. This perpetual framing of the unknown is neither bad nor good; it is inevitable. We all interpret what is happening around us through an invisible lens shaped by our history and social context.

PARADOXES OF GROUP LIFE

Earlier in this chapter, I mentioned an exercise where the instructor asked us to introduce ourselves from the perspective of someone who knew our shortcomings. While those introductions became more intense and personal as the group progressed, the first attempt was relatively benign—a woman shared a kindhearted introduction from her daughter's point of view.

At that point, our instructor discussed the Paradox of Disclosure. The paradox suggests, groups cannot evolve until individuals feel safe enough to share things they are afraid the others may reject.[6] In other words, a group cannot coalesce unless its members feel psychologically safe enough to be vulnerable.

My classmate's example was too safe to facilitate the group's development because there was no risk in her story. While she had bravely volunteered to go first, there was no chance the group would reject her. Therefore, the group could not bond as a result of the disclosure.

The Paradox of Disclosure comes from the book *Paradoxes of Group Life: Understanding Conflict, Paralysis, and Movement in Group Dynamics*, which breaks twelve paradoxes into three categories: belonging, engaging, and speaking.

Here is another example. Wall Street's example of wearing masks and her subsequent angry Black woman feedback represents the Paradox of Identity. "The group becomes strong and resourceful only if the individuality of its members can be expressed."[7] That is to say, groups are more robust when the members can be their authentic selves rather than conform to the group.

"Authenticity is a collection of choices that we have to make every day," according to Brené Brown. "It's about the choice to show up and be real. The choice to be honest. The choice to let our true selves be seen."[8] How can leaders facilitate this need for belonging and inclusion? While Wall Street took the well-intentioned criticism in stride, the feedback could have chilled psychological safety, not just hers but anyone in the group.

Maybe that group development experiment wasn't "artificial" after all. It helped me understand the discussion about where authenticity lives. The uncomfortable mirror check has pried me out of my shell and made me a better leader and person. If you are a leader, knowing why someone would follow you is key to managing a group. You cannot answer that question if you do not know the man in the mirror's reputation. His identity is irrelevant.

Dozens of proven personality inventories can help. You've likely taken the Myers-Briggs Type Indicator, a DISC assessment, the CliftonStrengths, the Predictive Index, or one of Hogan's assessments. Each of them will lump you into categories based on your disposition. Their value is in the subsequent self-reflection and what you do with that knowledge.

In a perfect world, Wall Street would not have to perform like a shapeshifter because of her gender and skin color. Society would accept her without all the masks she wears for us. We do not live in a perfect world. The most critical leadership lesson Wall Street taught me is that, as a white man, I should not be so sure of my reality. I should remain curious and remember that all individuals make sense of the same event through a unique lens that creates their reality. Others are products of their environment, too.

KEY CHAPTER TAKEAWAYS
- Leaders must seek opportunities to understand people's perspectives at the margins.

- Individuals make sense of the same event through a unique lens based on their lived experiences.
- Identity is how we view ourselves; reputation is how others view us. As a leader, your reputation determines whether people will follow you.
- Understanding your values, motivations, preferences, and biases allows leaders to be strategically aware of the signals they are sending.

CHAPTER 5:

THE MATTER OF GRAY MATTER

"The human brain is hardwired with a fervent desire to make sense of the world, to create connections between events whether they exist or not. From a rationalist's standpoint, it's something of a design flaw."

—BRAD PARKS

What role does fear play in leadership? Authority figures inherently hold power because they deliver rewards and reprimands. Therefore, employees will perceive risk anytime hierarchy is salient.[1] Humans are hardwired for self-preservation and to seek out community to make sense of their environment, minimize risk, and ensure survival. This chapter will explore how employees interpret leaders' signals from an evolutionary biology perspective. How leaders deal with this inherent challenge determines whether psychological safety can emerge.

Anthropologist David Scruton said, "If any human emotion is as old as our species, it must, surely, be fear, and the end of its hold on us is not in sight."[2]

Mr. Jones was a large man with thinning white hair and an endless grin. I frequently saw him walking near the A&W root beer stand. As a child peering out the back seat window, I caught a glimpse of him often enough that I was disappointed when he was not there. He was the first blind person I had ever encountered. I was in awe of how he navigated his darkness with only a perpetually moving white stick as a guide.

When I was about ten years old, I was shocked to find Mr. Jones at our house when I got off the school bus. He worked on pianos. My mother was taking up a new hobby, and her aunt's heirloom needed tuning. I discovered he had been one of Dad's veterinary clients for years.

One morning, Mr. Jones, his old silver Weimaraner, and his teenage son greeted my dad when he entered the exam rooms. A cat in the adjacent exam room let out a shrill screech during the dog's physical exam. Mr. Jones startled and let out a screech of his own. He was shuddering, obviously unsettled, and very stressed. As he began to regain his composure, Mr. Jones described how he had inadvertently stepped on a cat as a child, and it mauled his leg.

This fear seemed a new revelation to his son, or at least the spark for an ornery idea. The daydreaming teenager was suddenly paying close attention. As Mr. Jones recalled the childhood trauma, his progeny crept up behind him with a toothy grin and mimicked the sound of the cat that had sent chills down the older man's spine. At that moment, overcome with fight-or-flight adrenaline, Mr.

Jones whirled around and swatted the giggling teenager with his mobility cane.

Fear is an evolutionary emotion that evolved to protect us from threats; fear has not changed, but the modern-day threats we face have.[3] Additionally, people base much of their fear on a lifelong running tally of quasi-connected events.[4] Our survival instincts have taken us down the evolutionary path of *better to be safe than sorry* regarding real or perceived threats. Today, these instincts create frequent "false positives" about danger's presence.[5]

Mr. Jones's fear was palpable, and his response was understandable even though the danger was not real. We are navigating a sophisticated world with a defense system hardwired for our past when making snap decisions determining survival.

HEURISTICS AND BIAS

Our evolution to make snap decisions has created cognitive heuristics and biases. Heuristics are the mental strategies that attempt to simplify processing vast amounts of data because our cognitive resources are limited.[6] At the same time, biases are a tendency or prejudice in favor or against someone or something.[7] Our acquired knowledge and past experiences influence our sensemaking and are the foundation of these mental shortcuts and thinking patterns. It's crucial to recognize that heuristics and biases exist so leaders can mitigate their impact on sensemaking.

Why does it matter? Remember the discussion in chapter 3 of first impressions happening in the blink of an eye? Those first impressions are tough to change. This resistance to revision is a cognitive bias involving an overreliance on initial information called the "anchoring effect."[8] As a leader, you may make suboptimal decisions due to these shortcuts or mistakenly cling to your opinion about someone, even when their performance contradicts your belief—a belief formulated on a faulty or incomplete evaluation.

Researchers have cataloged two hundred types of cognitive bias, but we are unaware we are utilizing many of them.[9] You may have two equal candidates for a position. You can't figure out why, but you feel one would be the better contributor. You aren't consciously aware that they had a bumper sticker supporting your favorite team—but you *did* notice it when they got out of the car. Biases can be benign conscious choices, like our favorite food or color, or they can be harmful negative behaviors like overt racism.

Bias can affect decision-making when evaluating individuals or situations that don't fit preconceived notions. Our tendency to seek information confirming our preexisting beliefs or expectations is called confirmation bias. It can lead to uninformed decision-making because we fail to seek out or ignore contradictory evidence and tend to prioritize and retain information that confirms our preexisting beliefs.

Fear can exacerbate cognitive bias. For example, confirmation bias can lead employees to make sense of vague information in ways that confirm their suspicions. An illustration of this was my encounter with Beth in the introduction. When I failed to say good morning, Beth didn't know how to interpret the omission. She assumed I was mad at her for calling off.

When leaders rely on quick and easy-to-acquire information or give more credence to recent experiences when making decisions, they utilize availability heuristics. The availability heuristic occurs when we lack statistical knowledge and anticipate something will happen based on how we can recall similar events. Using these stand-ins can create a myopic perspective that overstates the importance of recent events and overlooks long-term concerns.

For example, we tend to overestimate the risk of shark attacks because they get a lot of attention and create vivid memories despite happening infrequently.[10] By ignoring less accessible but equally important information, we hamstring our ability to make informed decisions. I don't hesitate to get on a boat, but I get anxious swimming in the ocean. On average, five shark fatalities occur annually around the globe. At the same time, about four thousand recreational boating accidents result in an average of five hundred deaths each year in the US alone.[11]

As information spreads across a group or organization, it can influence others' perceptions and sensemaking. An availability cascade happens when a particular story or interpretation gains momentum or goes viral. It can create a collective bias as more people adopt it without considering its veracity.[12]

In *Give Me a Break,* John Stossel illustrated how the media's sensationalist coverage of shark attacks in 2001 fueled misconceptions. "Instead of putting risks in proportion, we [reporters] hype interesting ones. Tom Brokaw, Katie Couric, and countless others called 2001 the 'summer of the shark.'...In truth, there wasn't a remarkable surge in shark attacks in 2001. There were about as many in 1995 and 2000, but 1995 was the year of the O.J. Simpson trial, and 2000 was an election year. The summer of 2001 was a little dull, so reporters focused on sharks."[13]

In a work culture lacking psychological safety, we find a desire to avoid conflict and maintain harmony. Well-intentioned employees fail to challenge the status quo. This narrowing of perspectives and a failure to consider dissenting opinions is known as groupthink. It often occurs when people make decisions based on a desire to conform.[14] Consensus is a poor means of decision-making when it discourages alternative viewpoints and the critical thinking and constructive conflict necessary for the best options to surface.

It is important to recognize these cognitive shortcuts. While they help us understand our environments, they can also harm leadership by creating blind spots.

FEAR AS A MOTIVATOR

Innately, we recoil from the negative and are drawn toward the positive.[15] "Negative information or events have adaptive significance and lead to greater physiological arousal, trigger more cognitive processing, and are ascribed greater importance."[16] Research suggests it takes five positive events to balance out a single negative encounter,[17] that adverse events require more sensemaking than positive events,[18] and the need for sensemaking is more relevant in dysfunctional work cultures.[19] The implication for leaders is it may be more important to focus on what is working than what is broken.

There are better ways to motivate people than coercive leadership.[20] "As a society, we are still largely inured to a fear-based work environment," Dr. Edmonson says. "We believe (most of the time, erroneously) that fear increases control."[21] When leaders respond defensively or shut down challenging discussions, they discourage future contributions from those who question authority and chill the entire group.

Knowing what constitutes a negative response is difficult because everyone's trigger is unique. People are not blank slates when they join an organization. Life and work experiences shape their behaviors and perspectives. An individual's fears can reflect previous trauma and have little to do with present circumstances.[22] Creating psychologically safe work cultures is difficult—even for people-centric leaders—because psychological safety is fragile.

FEAR OF FAILURE

One of the most crippling fears organizations can help employees mitigate is the fear of failure. "Fear of failure can lead to a broad range of emotional and psychological problems, including shame, depression, anxiety, panic attacks, or low self-esteem," according to the Cleveland Clinic. "It may negatively affect how you perform at school or work, or how you interact with friends and family members."[23]

Employees may fear failure for a variety of reasons that are unique to each person. Some may fear losing their job or an opportunity for a promotion. Others may be perfectionists or worry that failing will make them look incompetent or unreliable in the eyes of others. The social pressure of falling short compared to a successful peer is a strong motivation to avoid failing.

When I managed the veterinary clinic, our medical records software had a summary chart showing every patient and the treatments due each hour. We hung a large flat-screen TV on a prominent wall in the ICU. The TV's purpose was to act like a beacon, signaling when the ICU team needed help. The chart reflected on-time treatments as green. If the team was behind schedule, treatments turned yellow, and eventually, if the system deemed them long overdue, they turned red. Leaders, doctors, or peers from another department could instantly see the team needed help.

In our dynamic reality, we had to rely on the team to triage and make decisions that saved lives. The display represented a plan for an ideal situation. Things were seldom ideal. We could run on-time treatment reports and hold technicians accountable for performance to the plan, but we never did. Sometimes, Fido's potty break happened at 5 a.m. instead of 3 a.m., and that was good even when it was red on the TV.

It likely meant the staff was living the mission of taking exceptional care of pets by prioritizing a seizing dog or helping save the dog who had been hit by a car.

For months after the TV's installation, people feared colors changing to red. Nobody wanted to be "in trouble" for getting behind.

We failed to recognize the unintended consequences of introducing a new technology into the system and did not appreciate the "social" dimension. Instead of being a visual signal for help, when people fell behind, they marked tasks completed because they didn't want to fail or be perceived as the weak link. Over time, the staff curbed the behavior as people trusted we would not use the monitor punitively, but initially, fear made the display virtually useless.

With our ingrained predisposition for self-protection, fear of failure can become rate-limiting and play a significant role in how individuals perceive, process, and respond to environmental cues.

Sara Blakely, founder of Spanx, became the youngest self-made female billionaire in history. She credits dinnertime conversations with her father for her success. Each day, he would ask Sara what she failed at. If there were no failures, he would be disappointed.[24] Focusing on failing big allowed Sara to understand failure is not an outcome but an opportunity. Not failing represents not stretching yourself far enough out of your comfort zone to be more than you were the day before.

Why aren't more lessons learned from failure shared across teams? Too often, leaders bury lessons in an HR file as part of a punitive review or accountability discussion. In a learning culture, people discuss failures. Employees see them as a valuable opportunity for growth and development. When all mistakes are handled punitively, rather than getting fewer failures, we only hear about them once they're too big to conceal.

ARE YOU FIXING PROBLEMS OR FIXING BLAME?

We must have accountability for deliberate violations, and it is okay to hold people to high standards, but leaders must be careful when assigning blame.

The first time I heard Dr. Edmonson speak, she shared a story about explaining the difference between blameworthy and praiseworthy failures to a group of business executives. Blameworthy failures are acts like deliberately choosing not to follow known protocols while praiseworthy failures happen due to acts of continuous improvement, experimentation, or hypothesis testing. When asked to consider this spectrum, the executives estimated that 2-5 percent of failures are blameworthy. The same executives estimated that their organizations treat 70-90 percent of failures as blameworthy.

Often, leaders need to go beyond the surface to understand the root cause of failures. Staffing the veterinary hospital's ICU was problematic. No model could account for the variability in labor demand between ailments. A ward full of stable patients could make for an easy day compared to a few critically sick pets needing near-constant hands-on support.

We attempted to mitigate the challenge by cross-training staff from other departments to supplement the team during volume surges. Imagine a scenario where everyone is working at capacity. No one has had time for a lunch break. It is a full ICU—an *all-hands-on-deck* kind of day—and a panic-stricken owner bursts through the emergency door with her dog who was just hit by a car in her arms. *Chaos!*

Who is to blame when a cross-trained new "technician" is pulled into the fray and gives a canine patient Prednisolone, which is only for cats, instead of Prednisone for dogs? Or maybe a vomiting patient received injectable Robaxin, which is a muscle relaxer, instead of Reglan for nausea.

These "failures" were rare, but were they a failure of the employee running into the burning building trying to help or a system failure? Were they blameworthy or praiseworthy? I was to blame for inadequately staffing the team or pushing untrained people into roles before they were ready.

COLLECTIVE SENSEMAKING AND WORK CULTURE

Relational leadership theory suggests an informal contract exists between leaders and employees. Each member has a continual opportunity to make sense of the relationship, and when it is advantageous, relationships act like mortar.[25] Three theories explain how sensemaking and relationships affect the culture-building process.

Social learning theory explains followers will mimic the behavior of leaders to ensure conformity to expected norms. A role-modeling process takes place when people view leaders as credible, and the employees begin to mirror the leader's thoughts, ideals, and behaviors.[26] Social Exchange Theory suggests people look at relationships through a subjective cost-benefit analysis lens.[27] It is based on the norm of reciprocity, a social convention that compels people to return a favor when someone has helped them.[28] Both parties remain satisfied if the relationship continues to be mutually beneficial.[29] Social identity theory explores how individuals fit as group members and their tendency to identify as part of the team rather than as individuals.[30]

In a work culture, psychological safety functions like a yoke in an airplane. When a pilot pulls a plane's yoke back, the aircraft rises. When they push the yoke forward, the nose of the plane dips. Leaders move a culture's yoke through the relationships they create and the meaning their behavior signals. When leaders exhibit supportive behaviors that develop inclusive relationships, perceptions of psychological safety increase, and the work climate improves. When leaders display dysfunctional behavior, it destroys psychological safety and has a detrimental effect on the culture. Leaders get to choose whether employees follow because they must, due to fear of reprisal, or, better yet, because they have been motivated by the leader's behavior.

KEY CHAPTER TAKEAWAYS

- Humans are hardwired to self-preserve and seek out community.
- Heuristics are mental strategies that attempt to simplify processing vast amounts of data because our cognitive resources are not unlimited.
- Biases are a tendency or prejudice in favor or against someone or something.
- There are better ways to motivate people than coercive leadership.
- Creating psychological safety does not mean managers have to be soft or overlook mistakes. Accountability is a critical part of a psychologically safe culture.

CHAPTER 6:

ABOUT-FACE

"There is nothing more difficult to take in hand, more perilous to conduct, or more uncertain in its success, than to take the lead in the introduction of a new order of things."

—NICCOLÒ MACHIAVELLI

As I sat out to complete my research, I wanted to find two comparison companies with contrasting work cultures. Finding a dysfunctional culture to study was straightforward. I got approval from a former employer to study a warehouse I had managed.

I identified three candidates for the exemplary company, but gaining access was challenging because I had no connections with decision-makers. I learned that letting a stranger in to research your work culture and publish the findings was viewed as a risk.

While trying to access an organization with a positive work culture, I began my research in the toxic distribution center. Subsequently, my former employer brought in a new leader whose approach was novel for the employees. They were viewed as allies, not adversaries, and were treated with dignity and respect. I abandoned looking for an exemplary company. Instead, I focused my research on the work culture that was evolving in front of me. I stumbled into a comparative case study in a single organization.

My former employer, a third-party logistics company I call 3PL, oversees warehousing for a large multinational consumer product corporation. I knew 3PL had chronically struggled with employee turnover and morale at its largest facility. When I contacted them, the opportunity to have me come back with fresh eyes intrigued them because problems were progressively getting worse. The organization recently fired an abusive leader, team morale was plunging, turnover was running more than 300 percent, and the location was losing money.

My research's main participants were blue-collar forklift operators. Their primary tasks consist of unloading trucks from the manufacturing plants, picking and staging outbound retail orders, and loading them on trucks. I was embedded in the operation for three and a half months. I completed more than one hundred hours of observations, informal interviews, and formal semi-structured interviews with the facility's leaders and frontline employees. I also administered a psychological safety survey.

I had access to the organization's corporate and local leaders, customer service employees, and human resource staff to provide context for the research setting. I reviewed historical data relating to productivity, turnover, and employee engagement. I also had access to weekly conference calls between 3PL and its customer to review the progress of the facility.

The customer demanded a quick turnaround, so the pressure on leaders was intense. This burden trickled down, and everyone sensed it. The facility showed classic symptoms of a toxic work culture: absenteeism, tardiness, turnover, low morale, distrust, apathy, and poor communication.[1]

As the new leader took the helm, I documented more supportive and encouraging behaviors. As I observed how the employees responded and the morale shifted, I had all the data I needed to answer my research question: What is the relationship between leadership behaviors and employees' perceptions of psychological safety?

BACKSLIDING

In 2008, 3PL's founder retired and sold the business to his leadership team. "When we bought the company, we thought we knew, and we really didn't. What I mean by that is you don't know what you don't know," the president told me in one of the interviews. "We were very good operators, but we weren't financial people, we weren't bankers, and we weren't accountants and things of that nature. So, could we operate a warehouse and operate a business? Absolutely. The mistakes we made were we overleveraged ourselves and didn't totally understand what we were getting ourselves into."

Resources were often in short supply because the business was cash strapped. Employees frequently lacked the necessary equipment to do the work. Leaders made difficult staffing decisions, resulting in layoffs and cutting employee benefits. The cuts are another example of competing values. Without the bold actions, 3PL may have folded.

With the benefit of hindsight, the president lamented some of the actions. As a leader, he suggested that he was ensuring sustainability, even if few people recognized it at the time. "At the end of the day, there is what I want to do and what I have to do, and they are not always the same," the president told me. "Unfortunately, that's life. Today, we're bigger, more sustainable, and on a better footing; we're more mature as a company."

The HR director explained the distribution center's problems began to spiral in 2014 when a long-tenured manager retired. A parade of incompetent facility managers replaced him. With all the leader churn in the manager role, 3PL's distal corporate leaders did not realize how bad the work culture in the warehouse was becoming and did not appreciate how much knowledge was leaving because employee turnover. For example, attrition made it challenging to find enough people well-versed in the legacy warehouse management system to train new hires and simultaneously keep up with the workload.

3PL's client had also been a detriment to its success in terms of recruitment, retention, and other staffing concerns. "If you rewind to the 2012–2014 period, we operated this building without a contract for the better part of two and a half years. The workforce knew it. We had a mass exodus of our tenured people," the HR director explained. Employees, especially those with families, were left with no choice but to depart the company in search of security. "If you know your current employer no longer has a long-term contract, and they are working on a month-to-month basis, at some point, you've got to look out for yourself."

The HR director remarked that the facility's average tenure for forklift operators went from 4.3 years to 2.1 years during this period. Performance plunged and inventory issues rose steeply as poorly trained employees hit the floor.

TOXIC LEADERSHIP

While employees struggled to find a footing in the organization, the leaders' behaviors were not helping. "When you treat people like shit, you get what we got," the corporate HR director told me. "Some of our leaders have not had a paradigm shift; they are still functioning like 'Do what I say because I said so.' Do what I say because I said so works in an environment where people have no choices. It works in an environment with a 12 percent unemployment rate. When you have to feed your family, and there is no way for you to make a living other than the job you have today, you are going to do what that guy says. When you are operating in today's environment, where you can walk out the door and have another job in five minutes, maybe even for more money than you are making, do what I said because I said so does not work."

For more than two years, an abusive facility manager, whom I will call Tom, prowled the warehouse. He frequently subjected operations supervisors to abusive behavior. "I overheard him one day telling one of them to put his foot in their asses out there," a customer service representative shared. "I mean, that's a little extreme, and he was always screaming at them in front of everybody."

A forklift operator confirmed these public humiliations. "He's talking to the supervisors, and they all come over with their tails between their legs, and like, man, there's no amount of money for me to walk around in their shoes."

The local HR coordinator described how Tom's behavior was a contagion for his supervisors. Dysfunctional behavior cascaded across the operation. No one was immune. "If you want respect, you have to give respect, especially when you are doing it in an open forum where other people can hear it because it trickles downhill," the HR coordinator said. "If a supervisor sees a manager treating people inappropriately or not being respectful, don't be surprised when, within a month, the supervisor is out there doing the same. You have pretty much made bad behavior acceptable."

Tom's outbursts were not reserved solely for members of his management team. A forklift operator remembered a scene at a shift start-up meeting where Tom swore at people and threatened to hold their paychecks if they did not comply with his demands. In another eruption, Tom called an impromptu all-hands meeting. "He stood on a chair in the breakroom. I thought he was going to have a stroke. I mean, veins popping out everywhere..." a forklift operator told me. "He was inviting people out to the parking lot. He was going to whip their ass."

The team experienced a sense of relief when Tom's reign finally ended. "He said he was coming in here to make a name for himself. Boy, he did. The single most positive thing I ever seen at the warehouse as a whole was the day he got fired. And that ain't no lie," an inventory control clerk said. "I mean, it was like angels sang. Everybody was in a good mood. They're like, things are going to change now."

3PL should have addressed the abusive leader much sooner and created a zero-tolerance policy for the type of behaviors he had normalized. In my interviews and observations, I saw ample qualitative data in the staff's stories to justify my claim that abusive supervision had created a toxic environment and employees lacked psychological safety. "People don't want to feel like this is a prison, which is what people were comparing it to," an operator told me. As I waited for the survey results, I wondered how much damage Tom's time at the helm did and whether the organization could overcome the residual effects.

A SAFE HARBOR

One of the fascinating things about psychological safety is that it can exist in microclimates within unsafe organizations.[2] During the darkest days at the distribution center, when many employees had all but given up, one supervisor, I will call Abner, became a buffer for the employees. He campaigned for necessary supplies, and he spoke up when people were mistreated.

It was no secret his authenticity and dedication were unique and translated to the frontline staff. Even with multiple supervisors on each shift, people still gravitated to Abner. His behavior was reciprocated with loyalty and productivity when those traits were in short supply. The HR coordinator said, "If we have four supervisors, and you know only one seems to care, you are going to go to him."

Abner's impact on the employees proves that you can lead regardless of your position in the organizational hierarchy. The supervisory role was his first real job after college. He had previous warehouse experience working in his family's business, and the challenge of a leadership opportunity at 3PL excited him. Still, as he acclimated to the new role, he quickly questioned his career choice. "There were times I just wanted to give up," Abner said. "I'm like, man, this can't be what the real world is like. This isn't normal."

When I asked why he persevered, he gave me two reasons. He was raised to finish what he started and felt a deep connection to the employees. Intuitively, he understood his role in providing them with a sense of optimism. "We're all family. More or less, we're here more hours than we are at home," Abner said. "Some of these operators are like they're my family because I hang out with them twelve hours a day, six days a week."

Abner had been with the company for fifteen months when I began my research. He got off to a rough start because he lacked some skills. People would come to him wanting help, and Abner did not have the software skills to solve their problems. Despite not having system competency, he quickly made progress with the employees by being empathetic, taking an interest in them, and developing relationships. "I mean, everybody's a person at the end of the day," he said. "You just gotta find the middle ground with everybody."

On one of my last days in the distribution center, I caught up with Abner to see how he thought things were progressing under the new leadership. Abner said he was glad he did not give up and quit. "It was very disheartening, but I just muscled through..." he said. "As much as people were like, man, this place is never going to change—look now. We've changed!"

Abner's experience reveals that psychological safety can exist in pockets, even in the most toxic environments. Leaders can look for opportunities to use authentic supervisors, like Abner, to help scale these microclimates across teams. Exposing more people to these supportive leaders, training on and modeling desired behaviors, and not tolerating toxic behaviors are strategies to foster psychological safety. Nothing will burn out a good employee faster than a manager tolerating a bad one. Work culture is defined by what leaders tolerate.

THE TURNAROUND

The HR director knew if 3PL were to have a reversal of fortunes, it would require a different approach. He needed to reframe the roles and expectations for all organizational leaders, beginning with the frontline supervisors. "If I asked any one of them, 'What is your primary responsibility as a supervisor?' I venture to guess most of them would say, 'Get the trucks loaded.' That's the problem. That is task management, not people management," he told me.

With that in mind, the HR director hired Jose to tackle the monumental task of turning around the distribution center. Jose had spent decades in logistics, and the director recognized his affable, people-centric approach might be a salve in Tom's wake. Immediately, people began responding. One of the operators explained that under Jose, "They actually ask us if we have any kind of input, and they don't make you feel bad about it. They'll tell you if you have an idea, try it. If it doesn't work, learn from it. But don't keep making the same stupid mistake. Learn from it and move on."

Eight weeks into his tenure, I sat down with Jose and told him he was getting a lot of credit for being the antidote for the ailing warehouse. I was curious if, when he joined the organization, he understood the scope of the facility's problem, what he attributed the recent operational success to, and what he thought about the evolution of the facility's work culture.

To 3PL's credit, Jose said they fully disclosed the challenge he would be facing. "Can you imagine if they'd tried to sugarcoat it... If you show up like it's just going to be business as usual, and you're walking through this place on day one, you're like, well, I'm glad I haven't unpacked because I'm out of here."

Jose humbly credited the employees who stuck with the company. "I've been really pleased with the way the team here has responded to our efforts," Jose said. "They could have just as easily told us, you know what, we've seen this too many times, for too long, we're going to stay jaded. You guys can just pound sand, and whenever you're gone, well, I guess we'll still be here for the next guy. But they really responded, and kudos to them for giving people like me another chance."

In this new environment, employees responded by engaging at a different level. They were more forthcoming with ideas and suggestions about how to fix problems. I witnessed forklift operators displaying more employee voice behaviors, which are discretionary and relate to how people contribute and communicate. The behaviors are often proactive and go beyond the requirements of a role. For example, employees frequently resolved or at least reported inventory problems; before, they usually just bypassed the issue. Even the general appearance of the facility changed as employees began picking up trash and fixing damaged inventory as they encountered it. The engagement was an indication that psychological safety was budding.

Jose said his job was easy after getting his team to understand his approach. Still, he had to do a lot of coaching because the supervisors had not yet aligned their behaviors with his, and some of the abusive behaviors lingered. To shift their paradigm, Jose would challenge them to explain when they had seen him modeling questionable behavior. It reinforced what he would tolerate and that he was leading by example. The supervisors grappled initially to come to terms with their new leader. "I was like, man, I don't really know this guy," one shared. "I can't even feel him out 'cause he's a hard-to-read guy, but you could tell that he's looking at everything, and he's just waiting to ask the right question at the right time."

Jose treated them respectfully, and his expectations were always realistic, but the team understood he held them to a higher standard. Eventually, the supervisors bought in. "It's just—it seems so simple. It's just his persona, just his presence," one supervisor explained. "He came in here, and he means business, and it looks like people are ready to work for him."

Jose's authenticity, consistency, and caring—like Tom's abusive behaviors—began to trickle down. The team's behaviors affirmed what everyone was hoping for. Things are changing. The path was not always clear, and the process encountered several challenges, setbacks, and disappointments, but Jose persisted. "If you're not sure of the problem, if you're not sure what to do, just do what you think in your heart is right, and then you figure out what's left," he said. "So that's kind of where we are right now. We've walked the walk. We're eight weeks in, and we are making the employees' lives better."

THE TIPPING POINT
Eventually, Jose's day-to-day leadership would likely have turned the culture around, but an impromptu event accelerated the timeline. A few months into his tenure, Super Bowl Sunday occurred. A Super Bowl is the type of event that historically derailed the operation for days. Employee call-offs created a backlog of work that could take weeks to dig out.

"I was worried about attendance on Super Bowl Sunday," the corporate HR director told me. "What did Jose do? He said, 'Look, guys, let's figure this out. You guys come to work as you are scheduled to work, and we will watch the second half of the game in the break room. It is on me.'"

"Do you know how many callouts he had? None," the director said. "Not only that. He came in on his day off and watched the game with them."

The HR director said many people would have taken a myopic view and focused on the short-term costs of paying fifty people to watch television for two hours. Jose understood it was money well spent because getting caught up after a mass callout event would have cost significantly more in overtime. He also understood the intangible benefit of generating goodwill and keeping the turnaround momentum going.

In addition to getting to watch the second half of the game, Jose placed anyone who worked their shift that day into a drawing for a $250 gift card. On the way to work, one of the supervisors won $100 on a scratch-off lottery ticket, so he bought pizza for everyone.

I asked Jose why he "hosted" a Super Bowl party. "The truth is, you ask anybody, and this is a huge deal. This is like one of the biggest social events of the year," Jose said. "It's the only thing that is not a national holiday that people really care about. I thought, you know, what can we do? It's unfair. I need them here. They have to be here. What's the middle ground?"

Jose was under a lot of pressure at the time. The distribution center's performance was finally improving, creating positive momentum, and rebuilding customer credibility. The facility could not afford a stumble. After calculating the hours and potential impact on productivity, Jose said it was the right decision for the operation. Still, even he was surprised by the effect it had on morale.

"Even if you weren't here and you just heard about it, you think people care about me as opposed to what they've usually got in store for us," one of the forklift operators told me. "That overrides a whole lot of stuff that has happened."

WHAT JUST HAPPENED

"I know the things you are researching are important, but it is just not in my vocabulary, and it is not something I understand," the company president told me as I concluded my research. "It is not in my DNA, but if you look at what we are doing, you have to account for how this new team is wired. I just can't comprehend how talking nicely to people and really giving a shit got us from there to here."

This research study's unique context—a turnaround environment—allowed me to investigate both the dark side of leadership behaviors that were detrimental to the work culture and destroyed psychological safety and the leader behaviors that rebuilt psychological safety and lifted the organization.

While specific leadership behaviors are contextual to an individual's needs, I needed something to measure leader behaviors that was widely applicable. I used the Servant Leadership Survey (SLS) that utilized eight behavioral dimensions of leadership.[3] While not all-encompassing, the dimensions are broad, replicable examples of supportive leader behaviors.

Dimension	Definition
Empowerment	A motivational concept focused on enabling people and encouraging personal development.
Accountability	Holding people accountable for performances that they can control.
Standing back	The extent to which a leader gives priority to the interests of others by giving them the necessary support and credit.
Humility	The ability to put one's own accomplishments and talents in a proper perspective.
Authenticity	Closely related to expressing the "True Self," expressing oneself in ways that are consistent with inner thoughts and feelings.
Courage	The ability to take risks and try out new approaches to old problems.
Forgiveness	The ability to understand and experience the feelings of others, and the ability to let go of perceived wrongdoings by not carrying a grudge into other situations.
Stewardship	The willingness to take responsibility for the larger institution and go for service instead of control and self-interest.

My research showed that psychological safety is significantly related to seven of the eight dimensions of servant leadership. Courage is the only dimension of these behaviors that was not statistically significant in my data. A possible explanation is when leaders show courage, employees may not recognize the behavior or have visibility to it.

Whether a conscious decision or just part of his affable nature, Jose's approach to leadership exemplified the behaviors used in my data analysis. He developed a new standard of accountability, demonstrated courage when he hosted an unauthorized Super Bowl party, and showed forgiveness and patience with employees as they struggled with the new leadership paradigm and increased expectations.

3PL had a long history of taking employees for granted and utilizing top-down management. As a former leader at 3PL, my boss never told me to make people's lives miserable. Yet I had to run mandatory seventy-two-hour work weeks. My boss never told me to be uncaring. Yet I was required to enforce a no-fault attendance policy, which did not account for family emergencies that left workers without childcare. It took courage for Jose to buck these historical norms.

At the outset, the employees' narrative accounts suggest they struggled to find sufficient stability to put down roots because of a chronic toxic work culture. In interviews, employees indicated the ambiguity they felt resulted from high turnover rates, constant change, inconsistent policy administration, and abusive leader behavior.

The rejuvenating behaviors like inclusiveness, humility, authenticity, and accountability changed the collective perception of psychological safety in the team. This turnaround shows that leaders' actions have consequences, and work cultures reflect leadership behaviors.

KEY CHAPTER TAKEAWAYS

- Psychological safety can exist in microclimates within an unsafe culture. The opposite is also true.
- Consistent accountability is crucial for developing psychological safety and high-performing teams.
- When employees perceive supportive behaviors like inclusiveness, humility, and authenticity, it builds trust and fosters psychological safety.

CHAPTER 7:

AIN'T DOIN' RIGHT

"The best doctor in the world is the veterinarian.
He can't ask his patients what's the matter.
He's just got to know."

—WILL ROGERS

Despite tagging along on farm calls and emergency visits as a kid, the industry was a mystery to me when I began helping my dad with projects at his veterinary clinic in 2014. Being thrown into the frantic pace of an emergency clinic was challenging. Learning the jargon and the acronyms, such as DKA, TPLO, and ADR, was like learning a foreign language. I quickly inferred ADR exams are for sick pets. I assumed ADR stood for something like Anonymous Disease Recognition.

Nope, the doctor is seeing your fur baby for an "Ain't Doin' Right" exam. It is a ubiquitous industry term.

Veterinary doctors and technicians go through a sensemaking process during an ADR exam as they try to diagnose why their patient ain't doin' right. The process is an excellent analogy for how leaders can support sensemaking. Here's an example of an ADR case.

Smokey, a three-year-old male neutered cat, was straining to urinate. Cats' urethra, the tube from the bladder to the outside, can become blocked due to inflammation and mucus plugs or crystals in the urine. When cats cannot urinate, it can be life-threatening. However, Smokey's examination and ultrasound did not reveal signs of being blocked.

Smokey's only symptom was straining, and his bladder was still small. So, he could still empty his bladder, and his urethra was not blocked. Thus, outpatient care was deemed appropriate, and the doctor prescribed medications to prevent urethral spasms and pain.

The patient returned to the emergency room two days later when his owner found him lying on his side, lethargic, and vomiting. Given Smokey's previous history, the first assumption was he was blocked. His bladder was still small and soft, ruling out this hypothesis.

In addition to being lethargic and unable to stand, the team noticed he appeared neurologically impaired. He responded to a stimulus but seemed confused. His third eyelids were elevated. Smokey had a low body temperature and was dehydrated. The immediate concern was that he had not eaten or drunk anything for days.

At our hospital, point-of-care testing (POCT) is part of every emergency appointment. POCT is a battery of rapid, reliable screenings that produce actionable results within minutes, which can aid in identifying and monitoring acute conditions or chronic diseases. Smokey's POCT did not reveal anything specific. His owner approved additional testing and hospitalization. In the ICU, the team monitored his hydration, temperature, and mental status around the clock. Despite assessing dozens of data points, they still had no diagnosis, so the sensemaking continued.

The doctor decided to test Smokey for a relatively common parasite that can cause toxoplasmosis, which could be responsible for the neurological symptoms. The test results take three to five days, but the treatment for toxoplasmosis is antibiotics and supportive care, which Smokey was already receiving.

That evening, Smokey coded—his heart had stopped beating, and he stopped breathing. The ICU team started Cardiopulmonary Resuscitation (CPR). They intubated the patient, began chest compressions and ventilation, and administered emergency drugs. After two rounds, they called the owner, who requested the staff discontinue CPR. A few days later, the lab results confirmed the toxoplasmosis diagnosis.

Veterinarians use a subjective, objective, assessment, and plan (SOAP) framework to create a medical record and make sense of this complicated diagnosis process.

Subjective data are general impressions based on observation. It can include observations subject to interpretation and cannot be measured.

Objective data, such as an animal's weight, are quantifiable and measurable and cannot be disputed.

The **assessment** is the doctor's opinion of the animal's condition based on analysis and differential diagnoses. The assessment includes things that the doctor has ruled out and identifies the problem(s) based on the subjective information and objective data previously collected.

The **plan** section includes a final diagnosis, immediate and long-term medical treatment plans, and client education. A short-term plan deals with day-to-day activities of feeding, care, and management of the animal's problems. The long-term plan facilitates communication and allows anyone reading the SOAP to understand the treatment.

What would happen if leaders applied the SOAP formula to help them "treat" the challenges they encountered in their organizations?

	Cat	Culture
Subjective	Lethargic Unable to stand Appears neurologically impaired	Palpable stress in the environment An absence of teamwork or cooperation, a toxic work environment, or unclear goals
Objective	Low temperature Elevated Third eyelids Dehydrated	Revenue per staff hour needs to be higher. Revenue per FTE veterinarian is low. Average client transactions are low. Client retention rate declining. Client wait times are excessive. Support staff turnover is high.
Assessment	Toxins and urethral obstruction have been ruled out	The organization lacks cognitive structural clarity and clear, concise communication from leadership. The organization needs leadership to establish clear workplace values and model behavior expectations. The team needs more leadership presence to support day-to-day operations and provide real-time direction. The clinic's schedule needs to align its resources with the service demand.
Plan	Pending toxoplasmosis test Hospitalization plan for stabilization	Clarify, communicate, and rally around the organization's purpose. Revise Key Performance Indicators to align with mission, vision, and values. Share one-year, three-year, and five-year organizational goals with employees. Review roles and job descriptions, ensuring they align with objectives and that people with the right skills are in the right roles. Clearly define and model desired behaviors. Invest in staff development by creating a robust training curriculum to fill the leadership skill gaps. Revamp schedule to match demand for services and expand capacity.

Think of the SOAP formula as another tool any manager could utilize regardless of industry. What I like about the "off-label" business use of the SOAP formula is that it helps separate emotion from fact, resulting in data-driven and logical decisions. However, the subjective data also ensures you keep track of the smallest component of the system—the individual employee's perspective.

I have been guilty of being too reliant on data. I was venting to a mentor about the difficulty of shutting out the employee drama at work. He reminded me, "Emotion is data too."

BURNING RUBBER

Dad often described his business partnership as "the second-best marriage I ever had." The partners were very successful, but I could argue they did it despite their relationship rather than because of it. The owners lived at opposite ends of the bell-shaped curve in many areas. Dad was too optimistic, impulsive, indifferent, and loose with details. His partner was cautious, calculating, empathetic, and meticulous.

They functioned like the pedals in my first car—a baby blue 1973 Ford LTD. I used to *burn rubber* by stomping on the brake and gas at the same time. It created a lot of noise and smoke, but I didn't get anywhere.

My first real taste of this dysfunctional stasis occurred at the "Tuesday morning meetings." This weekly leadership meeting between the two owners and the practice manager was a chance to review the current business and discuss things on the horizon.

After several weeks, I noticed the organization seldom completed projects. Leaders just shuffled priorities and focused on the hot button du jour. The same issues would cyclically come into heat. The business spent a lot of time roasting its tires.

Both men had a tremendous amount of respect for one another, and as a result, there was a lot of deferring. The two tap-danced around issues, but no one was driving change. When I finally sat down and captured all the open tasks, the project list exceeded forty items. The manager had too much on her plate to do anything but put out daily fires.

The practice had made a strategic decision to fill a market vacuum. It had expanded to twenty-four-hour emergency care. Immediately, the clinic began receiving referrals from other veterinarians, and within a few years, the practice had more than doubled its revenue and staff. It had grown to nearly one hundred employees, but no one was focused on talent optimization or providing human resource support.

Although the clinic was growing, it was not healthy. The veterinary industry defines a business like this as a "No-Lo Practice," meaning it has little or no market value because of its poor profitability relative to its gross revenue.

Dad told me, "We are taking care of the patients and the staff, but no one is looking out for the owners." I was determined to change that.

We tore the business down to the studs. I hired an industrial/organizational psychology master's graduate, and we developed an HR system, focused on building leadership depth, and implemented organizational infrastructure to create a stable foundation.

DO HARD THINGS

One of Dad's favorite stories was about a colleague who employed a toxic receptionist for years. The veterinarian confided, "Every day, I wake up, and I'm so excited. I race into work, hoping this will be the day she has finally quit." Veterinarians get to save lives, fix broken bones, and be the hero. That is much more gratifying than dealing with an employee with an attendance issue or someone whose negative behavior affects team morale. It is easier to do your business than run your business.

Despite my lack of industry knowledge, I started seeing many of the same problems and patterns I had dealt with in my logistics career. The people problems were the same: poor communication, lack of role clarity, budgetary limitations, and staff feeling unappreciated. I remember some of our early discussions about the clinic's culture. Employee apathy and negativity were chronic problems. Ironically, the operational issues were often the same: unpredictable dynamic volume, training deficiencies, workflow bottlenecks, and schedule waste.

No one was willing to make fundamental decisions. Even when owners made decisions, they often capitulated to staff resistance, and projects died. The leaders hesitated to push too hard for fear of losing vital contributors. The owners felt stuck and resigned to fate, which left them frustrated, the business erratic, and the staff feeling like the management approach was *ready, fire, aim.*

Our schedules were inefficient. Since this hospital was a twenty-four-hour facility, it didn't close for a typical one-hour lunch break. A daily task was determining when people took lunch, whether people could even get a break, and in what order people left the floor. It should be a strategic decision based on patient care, available resources, and collective skill set—not fear of making a coworker unhappy.

Long-tenured technicians worked banker's hours and were gone by 4 p.m. Due to the new emergency service, the clinic's busiest time was between 4 p.m. and 7 p.m. Only a junior varsity team remained when critical patients arrived from referring hospitals at crunch time.

The dysfunctional staffing went beyond the support staff. Management routinely scheduled five doctors on Tuesdays, one of our lowest volume days. On Sundays, when we were the only clinic open in southern Illinois, a single doctor was planned because no one wanted to work weekends.

The clinic paid its veterinarians on a production-salary basis (Pro-Sal is a commission-based model). The theory is "You kill it; You eat it." It is a win-win meritocracy because a doctor's paycheck directly reflects the revenue they generate. It is a great system when the schedule aligns with demand. However, when doctors had nothing to do, like on any given Tuesday, it created a cut-throat environment.

While everyone was focused on taking exceptional care of pets, the imbalanced schedule hampered collaboration and created competitive hostility among some professional staff.

The culture was a house of cards built on "gentle reminders" and prioritizing harmony. We were reaping what had been sown. Our challenges were a byproduct of letting things happen rather than making them happen. The things you tolerate define your culture.

I was dealing with these problems during my pre-enlightened and still functioning with a top-down mindset. I was pushing for change—hard—leaving the staff unsettled.

Then the practice manager quit unexpectedly. She was the face of the clinic and irreplaceable in many ways. She had been with the clinic for more than thirty years. Starting in the boarding kennels, she had advanced to the top of the organization. She and her decades of intellectual capital were gone. The vacuum pulled me deeper into the organization than anyone ever intended. Overnight, I became the de facto practice manager.

I leaned heavily on data and focused decision-making around our mission: "We take exceptional care of pets." The statement became more than a slogan. It was the lens through which I viewed all decisions. Should we buy a new piece of equipment? Does it help us take exceptional care of pets? Should we add an extra technician during peak hours? Does it help us take exceptional care of pets? Should we send two ICU technicians to lunch together because it is Cindy's birthday? Does it help us take exceptional care of pets?

I cared deeply about our employees, but that is not what my behavior reflected. As a leader, I focused on the business objectives and viewed other considerations as subordinate. I reasoned that if I could make the business healthy, there would be more resources for everyone. At the time, I had not heard of psychological safety. I didn't understand how my behavior contributed to the challenges the clinic was experiencing.

A WATERSHED MOMENT

One of my first projects was to "make the schedule match the census." We had to choose between doing something unpopular with the staff—some on the leadership team viewed changing the schedule as "messing with people's lives"—or living with the status quo, which limited our mission's effectiveness and the organization's health. It was clearly in the best interest of our patients, clients, and business to change.

I had to align the workforce with the demand for our services, not the staff's preferences. Like an artificial intelligence management bot, I created a schedule void of individual considerations. It rotated like a two-two-three manufacturing schedule, which is entirely equitable. I grouped doctors into pairs working opposite days, which enhanced ICU patient rounding and communication.

One of the doctor pairs came into my office immediately after I published a sample schedule. They were very agitated because the constructed schedule did not work for their circumstances. As a parent with a young child, I was empathetic.

I reiterated why we were changing and all the benefits to patient care. The schedule was just an example. They had the autonomy to modify it as needed. The doctors returned a short time later and sheepishly gave me a proposal. They said it met my outlined scheduling parameters and solved their work-life balance problems. I approved it.

As we transitioned from a tail-wagging-the-dog schedule to one that prioritized the business, people struggled to accept the new model and my leadership. During a staff meeting, I made a critical communication gaffe. The staff understood the schedule benefitted the patients, the clients, and the organization. However, I had not convinced them at the level of *what was in it for me*. The schedule's twelve-hour shifts meant some people might not see their young kids three days a week.

I attempted to frame the discussion around how making the organization healthier would benefit all stakeholders. I suggested accomplishing these goals meant "our new priorities must be the patient, the client, the enterprise, and the staff—in that order."

The team heard, "They don't care about us. They don't value us." Looking at my message from their perspective, I see how being listed as the fourth priority could lead to feeling unappreciated. The toothpaste was out of the tube, and there was no quick fix to get it back in.

In the introduction of this book, I shared a Bakhtin quote. "Language lies on the borderline between oneself and the other. The word in language is half someone else's."[1] It did not matter what I intended or whether the efficiencies would allow us to provide better benefits and increase wages. I destroyed any goodwill I had built by not communicating on a level that supported individuals.

We chose—or maybe I bulldozed into existence—the unpopular schedule. It took time, but ultimately, our schedule matched the census and reflected our business priorities. It aligned with client demand, created capacity, eliminated waste, and delivered cost savings. Addressing the infrastructure problems was the first step in correcting why the business *Ain't Doin' Right*. Fixing a toxic culture is essential, but it is a moot point if the company is not sustainable.

Months later, one of the *agitated* veterinarians approached me. She thanked me and said, "I am making more money and working fewer hours than ever." Trickle-down economics often fail, but the increased efficiency and additional revenue did benefit everyone. We were able to raise wages and enhance benefits significantly.

In hindsight, I would have been more transparent in addressing the staff's concerns about *what's in it for me*. The risk was over-promising and underdelivering on their compensation and benefit bonanza. Minimizing the resentment and animosity during the transition would have justified the risk.

I remained with the clinic for six years, and I'd like to think I recovered from communicating employees were not a priority, but I'm not sure. Will Rogers also said, "You never get a second chance to make a good first impression."

COMPASSION FATIGUE

I know this is a generalization, but most people do not get into the veterinary field to get rich. If they do, they are quickly disappointed. Many vets face crippling student debt, and it is hard to make the economics of practice ownership work. Veterinarians invest in the same cutting-edge technology used in human hospitals but only charge a fraction of what human healthcare does. Only about 3 percent of the North American pet health insurance market is realized.[2] A 2022 survey revealed that 36 percent of all Americans have no savings, and another 19 percent have less than one thousand dollars saved for emergencies.[3] That leaves a lot of furry, feathery, and scaley loved ones exposed.

The nature of a veterinary hospital exacerbates the problem. Like the ADR example at the beginning of this chapter, veterinarians cannot save every pet. What happens when a young family shows up with an energetic new puppy that fell off the couch and needs a two-thousand-dollar fracture repair? Too often, the outcome hinges on money. People get into the field because they are passionate about the human-animal bond, not haggling for cash. For many, caring so deeply about their job is a privilege and an affliction. Imagine the emotional toll on a veterinarian who has the superpower to fix Fido's broken leg but doesn't have the resources. At times, it felt like economic euthanasia was the leading cause of death in our emergency hospital.

We compounded this emotional toll when we decided to support the pet-owning community in their time of need by allowing walk-in end-of-life care. Our logic was that knowing when the time is right is hard. So, we opted to be there regardless of when the time was right—whenever people mustered the courage to say goodbye.

I returned from lunch one day and met our medical director in the parking lot. She looked broken. When asked if she was okay, she said, "I have to leave here for a while. I just did my eighth euthanasia of the day."

COLLATERAL DAMAGE

Imagine being a veterinarian and watching a conversation where Mom told the kids they didn't have money to fix the puppy's leg. While giving them privacy to say their goodbyes, you decide to check on your patient in the ICU. The technicians are short-staffed due to a call-off, and the ones there are dealing with an emergency. Your patient has not received their medication and is in obvious pain. Understandably, doctors sometimes snap.

Early in my tenure, I coached a doctor who was "hard on the staff." Management had warned her before, but she continued berating and upsetting technicians. As we discussed the most recent tear-inducing event, she said, "I keep hearing management talking about the mission to take exceptional care of pets. That is exactly what I'm trying to do." From her perspective, the staff was being too thin-skinned, and she didn't have time for "pleasantries."

At the time, I agreed with her. She promised to be kinder to the staff, and the conversation ended. I thought of it as collateral damage. After all, our most talented, most passionate, and highest-earning doctors were generally the ones involved in these stress fractures. Our compensation structure created competing values. Why would we tell a rainmaker to take their foot off the gas? The organizational precedent was not to bite the hand that feeds you, so leaders ignored these eruptions.

As I moved through my program and researched psychological safety, I understood the outsized role (formal and informal) leaders' behavior has on work cultures. I realized it was untenable to continue to allow these toxic interactions. In hindsight, the veterinarian's singular focus on patient care reminds me of the phrase "reality distortion field" that Apple employees use to describe Steve Jobs' refusal to accept limitations and obstacles that got in the way of his innovations.[4] I realized the veterinarians' zeal for healing their patients prevented me from rehabilitating mine—our organization's culture.

One approach to veterinary medicine is called Fear Free. The objective is to alleviate fear, anxiety, and stress in pets during their appointment. It uses practices like minimizing restraint, giving medication to help pets relax, and employing pheromones to increase feelings of security. The least we could do was provide our staff with a fear-free work culture. As we worked through changes, some doctors moved on; others curbed the counterproductive behavior.

COMPETING VALUES
It felt like we were coming through the rapids and headed toward smooth water. Then the pandemic hit. On March 24, 2020, we divided the entire organization into two teams.

One team came in the front as the other exited the back door. We were concerned a positive coronavirus test would shut down the vital services we provided our community. If one team had an infection, we could subdivide the remaining team and at least provide emergency care with skeleton crews.

A few months later, after reviewing guidance from the health department, we realized our contingency plan was excessive. When we tried to return to a schedule with blended teams, some of the staff pushed back. People were scared and rightfully so. We were dealing with a novel virus, and no one knew what to expect. The staff could not articulate the source of their fear, and I couldn't mitigate an unknown risk. In the meantime, our mission was suffering.

We were encountering scenarios that threatened patient safety. For example, a new graduate was at the end of a long overnight shift and doing a complex emergency surgery for the first time. The result was the patient spent more time under anesthesia, which increased the safety risk. One of the top surgeons in the area was in the parking lot and was available to help but could not scrub in and mentor or take over due to the COVID protocols we had in place. The more I pushed to change our COVID protocols, the more the staff pushed back.

This impasse exemplifies competing values choices leaders often face, as well as the inherent tension between organizational priorities and maintaining harmony.[5] Leaders must make decisions and implement organizational policies that directly and indirectly affect employees.[6] Sometimes, the choices are decisions like: Does a leader focus on profit or sustainability? Do they focus on quality or efficiency? Other times, the impact is more direct: Do I pay vendors or cut 401K contributions? Do I fail to meet the customer's expectations or run mandatory overtime?

Perceptions of psychological safety are susceptible to distal leader decisions. Researchers have found that employees must maintain a sense of cohesion and avoid becoming lost in the ambiguity of change.[7] Their findings suggest that employees must feel their status is safe throughout the process for change to become ingrained. No one felt safe during COVID.

I completed my doctoral program during the pandemic. Plans for my departure had been in the works for months. We mutually decided that, like when a sports team struggles, it was time for a new leadership voice in the clubhouse. I left at the end of 2020. I was blessed to work with some fantastic people and have a learning laboratory to watch psychological safety ebb and flow. I left the organization better than I found it. Financially and structurally, it was healthier, but culturally, it still felt like the hospital *Ain't Doin' Right*.

People use terms like slog or ground war to describe the hard work of communication and culture change. I appreciate the imagery of a ground war, but using it in a business context disparages our troops. However, the Navy SEALs have an appropriate phrase to describe what must be done to change a work culture, "Embrace the suck."

What we did during my time at the clinic, the continuous improvement and relentless pursuit of practicing cutting-edge medicine, was arduous. Lots of tears were shed in the name of change. Knowing what I know today, I would have pursued the same agenda but been cognizant of the shadow my behavior cast. The premise of this book—leader behavior affects employees' psychological safety—is borne out of my lived experiences, which were often failures.

How a work culture evolves is based on whether a leader's behaviors enhance or undermine employees' psychological safety. Leaders must do hard things, but how they do them matters.

KEY CHAPTER TAKEAWAYS

- Emotion is data, too. Subjective data also ensures you do not lose track of the system's smallest component—the individual employee's perspective.
- Leaders must do hard things. The enterprise's well-being suffers when leaders fail to rise to these challenges.
- What a leader communicates does not matter; only what the employee hears matters.

CHAPTER 8:

MORE THAN A THEORY

"We've paid people for their hands for years, and they would've given us their heads and their hearts for free if we had just known how to ask them."

—BOB CHAPMAN, CHAIRMAN AND
CEO AT BARRY-WEHMILLER

My son began studying karate at Goshen Martial Arts in kindergarten. He showed up two or three nights a week for six years and practiced forms, self-defense techniques, and sparring. His journey culminated in sixth grade when he received his black belt. Although he has moved on from martial arts, we both took away lifelong lessons.

The academy's students were diverse. There were big students and small students. Some were young, others old. Some were athletic; a number were frail. At each belt promotion, the playing field leveled. The students had to demonstrate mastery of their skills by breaking a board at a promotion ceremony. Success was more about technique than physical attributes. Performing in front of their peers and their peers' families amplified the pressure of the board break.

Students recited a creed at the beginning of every class: "With strength and perseverance, I will battle through adversity and overcome all challenges. My attitude is everything, and my character is who I am. I am a martial artist!"

The academy's master told me, "I think the creed is an important affirmation, so we have the students say it when they break boards, join a more challenging class, or receive feedback on what they can do better. This way, they can approach the challenge with confidence in themselves."

When the students are new, they often pull their punches or kicks, fearing the pain of striking the hard surface. As they gain experience, they learn to trust their techniques and confidently strike through the board.

Early on, the boards are twelve inches long, three inches wide, and a half-inch thick. They are cut against the grain and snap easily with solid contact. As students progressed and their skills become more advanced, the boards become wider and more challenging to break. At my son's last belt promotion, the board was ten inches wide, and he had to break it with a jump-spinning back kick. That not only meant that the board was more robust but that he was kicking the board while in mid-air, and because he was spinning, he had to hit a blind target.

At the promotion ceremonies, students warm up on a soft hand target a few times and receive last-minute instructions. Then the moment of truth: The instructor braces themselves and grasps the boards at opposite ends as the crowd begins cheering and clapping. The instructor commands "Sijak," the Korean word for begin. A flurry of action and a crisp snapping sound of the board breaking signifies success—but not always.

Occasionally, students need more than one attempt.

"Sijak."

The student gets fidgety.

"Sijak."

The student starts to flush.

"Sijak."

The student becomes emotional.

"Sijak."

The instructor's knuckles turn white as they apply increasing pressure to facilitate the board splitting.

"Sijak."

With each failed attempt, the crowd grows louder, the clapping more vigorous, and my vicarious embarrassment intensifies. I feel a cold sweat coming on and the need to look away.

"Sijak."

At last, a clean strike and a crisp snap.

The academy taught students resilience and perseverance; skills equally valuable as the martial arts they mastered. The rest of us witnessed psychological safety, which is "a shared expectation held by members of a team that teammates will not embarrass, reject, or punish them for sharing ideas, taking risks, or soliciting feedback."[1] Students took risks every time they walked onto the mat. The academy is a supportive learning environment; failure is a valuable part of the process.

What would happen if everyone worked in that kind of work culture?

BARRY-WEHMILLER

Bob Chapman authored the 2015 Wall Street Journal Bestseller *Everybody Matters: The Extraordinary Power of Caring for Your People Like Family.* In an interview published on the Michigan Ross website, Chapman's alma mater, he was asked why he wrote the book. "We want to spread our message that business can be a powerful force for good if we simply learn the skills of caring for others," Chapman said. "We want people to see that if Truly Human Leadership can happen in an industrial manufacturing company, it can work in any company."[2]

This chapter considers why Bob Chapman, former CEO of Barry-Wehmiller, exemplifies the leadership behaviors that foster psychologically safe cultures I advocate for in this book. It examines Chapman's approach to leading, engineering culture, and succeeding. Chapman assumed control of his family's small manufacturing business in 1975 after his father died suddenly. He did what most business schools teach; he focused on controlling expenses and increasing profits. He leveraged people to create shareholder value. Eventually, Chapman's philosophy shifted.

In 2002, Chapman and his team created Barry-Wehmiller's Guiding Principles of Leadership (GPL). This leadership philosophy prioritizes employees' well-being and personal growth. "These are the fundamentals of leadership we should never forget," Chapman says in *Everybody Matters*. "Everything we do in the future needs to be in harmony with these principles."[3]

Barry-Wehmiller
Guiding Principles of Leadership

We measure 'success' by the way we touch the lives of people.

- A clear and compelling vision, embodied within a sustainable business model, which fosters personal growth.

- Leadership creates a dynamic environment that
  - is based on trust
  - brings out & celebrates the best in each individual
  - allows for teams and individuals to have a meaningful role
  - inspires a sense of pride
  - challenges individuals and teams
  - liberates everyone to realize "true success."

- Positive, insightful communication that empowers individuals and teams along the journey.

- Measurables allow individuals and teams to relate their contribution to the realization of the vision.

- Treat people superbly and compensate them fairly.

- Leaders are called to be visionaries, coaches, mentors, teachers, and students.

- As your sphere of influence grows, so grows your responsibility for stewardship of the guiding principles.

We are committed to our employees' personal growth.

Bob Chapman - Barry-Wehmiller

Rhonda Spencer - Barry-Wehmiller

Bob Leonard - Accraply

Chris Manley - Design Group

Jim Meier - Design Group

David Brown - Fleetwood

Zak Volz - Fleetwood

Jamie Asbury - Hayssen

Mike May - Hayssen

Julie Podmolik - MarquipWard

Diane Salvarola - MarquipWard

Jeff Shilts - MarquipWard

Maureen Schloskey - MarquipWard

Bob Valenti - MarquipWard

Adam Brandt - Pneumatic Scale

Mark Zaiden - Pneumatic Scale

Thiele Technologies

Donn Boyer - Thiele Technologies

Mark Prak - Thiele Technologies

John Beeler - Zepf

Bill Sharp - Zepf

Rhonda Spencer, Barry-Wehmiller's Chief People Officer, described what happened after a small team of people went into a room with Chapman to reimagine the business and emerged with a cultural vision statement, "We just went away to have a conversation about what was happening...people started talking, and I just started typing, and we ended up with some truths that we all agreed on about the way we would want a place to be to work."[4]

When HR shared the GPL document within the organization, an employee emailed Spencer the values statement used by Enron. It read, "We treat others as we would like to be treated ourselves. We do not tolerate abusive or disrespectful treatment. Ruthlessness, callousness and arrogance don't belong here."[5] Enron did not live out its values. It had become infamous for ethical failures. Its leaders abused their power, misrepresented information, and put their interests above those of their stakeholders.

These deviant behaviors ultimately led to the company's demise and its CEO spending twelve years in federal prison. When Chapman saw Enron's value statement, he committed that the GPL would represent Barry-Wehmiller's lived values. He said, "We're going to take those off the wall and put them into the hearts and minds of people," according to Spencer.[6]

The central idea of *Everybody Matters* is prioritizing employees' well-being will lead to better business outcomes. When everybody matters, everybody wins.

As people made sense of the supportive, empathetic, and caring behaviors that Chapman and his team exhibited, employees perceived leaders as authentic and trustworthy.

Barry-Wehmiller's employees rewarded the leaders with what researchers have called organizational citizenship behaviors. These behaviors go beyond the scope of regular job duties and provide significant value to the organization.[7] It could be something as simple as picking up trash left in the break room or something more impactful like volunteering an idea for a process change that could enhance safety, increase productivity, or reduce waste. It is the opposite of a *that's not in my job description* mentality. These behaviors go unrecognized in many organizations, but at Barry-Wehmiller, they began to celebrate and reward this discretionary behavior.

Chapman and his team fulfilled the aspiration of putting the GPL into people's hearts and minds. "We can say whatever we want," Spencer said. "We can put whatever we want on the wall, but my culture at Barry-Wehmiller is how my leader treats me."[8]

TEACH A MAN TO FISH
Spencer said some of the distinctive learning environment DNA was present even in the old days before Barry-Wehmiller's culture was exceptional. "I always joke that back then, if you had a brain, a pulse, and ambition—not necessarily in that order—people

would just let you try things. And it is really something that shaped how I think about what Barry-Wehmiller should be today."[9]

In 2006, Barry-Wehmiller began evaluating lean manufacturing. Lean is a production process focused on eliminating waste and maximizing output. As Chapman explains in his book, "When people hear that, they worry that *they* might be considered part of the waste that gets eliminated."[10] What Chapman described as the "real power" of lean was it created a process for listening to employees and validating their expertise and contributions.[11]

Matt Whiat, Founding Partner at Chapman & Co. Leadership Institute, told me, "The whole reason we went down this road of listening and all of this stuff was process improvement. When we were using the tools of lean, we realized our people didn't actually know how to listen to other people." The institute was founded in 2015 to share Chapman's teachings and Barry-Wehmiller's cultural transformation with businesses worldwide.[12]

With this new insight into the communication gap, leaders doubled down on training the organization to listen actively. Then they focused on the people closest to the problems solving them. The dalliance with lean resulted in the Living Legacy of Leadership program (L3). Think of L3 as a lean remix that prioritizes the team members' work life with reduced waste and improved productivity being byproducts rather than the focus of the process.[13]

In 2007, Barry-Wehmiller launched its internal training program (Barry-Wehmiller University—BWU) to scale L3's knowledge and help all team members toward self-actualization. On the podcast, Spencer explained the evolution of BWU and how the team developed its content. "We put Post-it Notes up on the wall of all the stuff Barry-Wehmiller Leaders should be, know, and do. We boiled that down and decided to focus on front-line leaders. That's where culture happens."[14]

The internal program emphasizes leaders actively and empathetically listening because when employees feel heard, they know they matter. In a blog post on the company website, Chapman explained, "Unlike many corporate training experiences, the goal of the class is not to 'get more out of' our team members, but rather to teach them the fundamentals of leadership, so they might positively impact the lives of others in their roles as leaders."[15]

When Chapman advocates for "Truly Human Leadership," he emphasizes the uniqueness of each employee. The approach hinges on building a supportive and compassionate workplace culture so employees can leverage their talents and fulfill their aspirations. What differentiates Barry-Wehmiller's approach is Chapman's mandate to help people flourish both at work and in their lives at home. Chapman's philosophy expands the scope of a leader's responsibility beyond the walls of Barry-Wehmiller. Leaders should see themselves as stewards of their employees' lives. A leader must care for the well-being of employees, their families, and the community.[16]

SYSTEM TEST

The 2008–2009 economic downturn—triggered by the collapse of the US housing bubble—tested Chapman's approach. Barry-Wehmiller found itself in a precarious cash flow position when the crisis led to a 40 percent drop in new equipment orders. Just as Chapman felt the people-first culture was starting to take root, he faced the prospect of laying off many of the employees he had committed to impact their lives positively. "I asked myself, 'What would a caring family do when faced with such a crisis?'" Chapman said. "The answer soon came to me: All the family members would absorb some pain so that no member of the family had to experience dramatic loss."[17]

Rather than facing layoffs like many in the US workforce, Chapman devised a furlough program where employees would take four weeks of unpaid time off and share the cost-cutting burden. He credits this act of walking his talk with converting the skeptics and fence sitters who resisted buying into the cultural transformation. The shared burden galvanized the organization, and Barry-Wehmiller's business recovered quicker than the rest of the US economy.

Chapman's approach to people-centric leadership mirrors the definition of servant leadership. In Robert

Greenleaf's seminal work, *Servant Leadership: A Journey into the Nature of Legitimate Power and Greatness:*

"The Servant-Leader is servant first....The best test, and difficult to administer is this: Do those served grow as persons? Do they, while being served, become healthier, wiser, freer, more autonomous, and more likely themselves to become servants? And what is the effect on the least privileged in society? Will they benefit, or at least not further be harmed?"[18]

In *The Lean CEO: Leading the Way to World-Class Excellence*, Chapman explains his servant leadership approach. "When somebody comes into our organization and agrees to join us, when we invite them into our organization, we become stewards of that life, just as we are when a child comes into our life. A different level of intensity but the same concept. And the way we treat that person who joins our organization will profoundly affect that person's marriage and the way that person raises their children and interacts with our community."[19]

SCALING EXCELLENCE

Barry-Wehmiller has scaled its unique approach to managing human capital. Since defining the GPL, Barry-Wehmiller has been in growth mode. It has a track record of acquiring and transforming struggling businesses into profitable assets. In isolation, what happened with Barry-Wehmiller's culture would be impressive, but it would be a single data point. As Barry-Wehmiller grew, each merger or acquisition created a laboratory to experiment on how to live the mission of positively impacting employees' lives. Barry-Wehmiller has introduced the GPL to 130 acquisitions.

In 2009, Chapman's son, Kyle, cofounded the private equity firm BW Forsyth Partners. It combines private equity experience with the people-centric approach to value creation. "We thought there was an opportunity to take the skill sets we developed—that my dad's team developed—combine it with a traditional private equity model," Kyle told the Olin Family Business Symposium. Forsyth focuses on "long-term, buy, build, and hold—invest in what you know—and build great companies' people are proud to be associated with, to work in, and send their people home fulfilled."[20]

The traditional private equity model focuses on increasing profitability, often at employees' expense, and then flipping the acquisitions to make a quick buck. According to its website, Forsyth takes a unique approach: "With every company we acquire, our goal is to buy, build and keep on building, alongside the talented people who make the business possible. Because companies don't create value; people do."[21]

Chapman's leadership philosophy has been proven time and time again. Often, the benefits of people-centric leadership are intangible and hard to quantify. However, in the aggregate, it is hard to argue his approach. When Chapman took over after his father died in 1987 the Barry-Wehmiller Company was a small local manufacturer doing twenty million dollars in revenue. Today, the company is a three-billion-dollar-plus global leader providing diverse products to dozens of industries.[22]

Between Barry-Wehmiller and BW Forsyth Partners, Chapman has implemented his distinctive value creation and culture transformation philosophy more than 160 times. All but a few have flourished. The outliers represent the adage that *there can be no mission if there is no margin.* "If you can't turn it around financially, we have never been able to turn around the culture either," Whiat told me. "We have never sold any of our acquisitions....If we take it, it is on us to make it work, and if we can't make it work as a standalone separate company, it will get absorbed within the greater Barry-Wehmiller architecture."

The commitment to people has become a hallmark of Barry-Wehmiller and BW Forsyth Partners' M&A activity and a differentiator for firms considering a union.

I have read *Everybody Matters* twice, and I don't recall any mention of psychological safety. By design, the leadership curriculum taught by Barry-Wehmiller is original material that evolved organically. "We decided that we would develop our own material because we wanted it to be distinctively Barry-Wehmiller, evocative of our unique worldview that you couldn't get anywhere else," Chapman says in *Everybody Matters.*[23]

The fact that psychological safety is not part of Barry-Wehmiller's lexicon is inconsequential. The leadership team at Barry-Wehmiller exemplifies the behaviors that foster psychological safety outlined in this book.

- They lead ethically and build inclusive relationships with their team.
- They actively listen and are clear and consistent in communicating information.
- They have created learning environments encouraging experimentation, continuous improvement, and intelligent failure.
- They take a systems approach that focuses on the smallest unit of the organization—the employee.

Barry-Wehmiller employees receive cues from their leaders that enable them to move beyond trusting leadership to feeling psychologically safe, which can unleash the best version of each employee.

TOO MUCH OF A GOOD THING

One misconception about psychological safety is that it creates a lack of accountability because it is about being warm and fuzzy. As discussed throughout this book, accountability is critical for people to feel they are being treated justly, for clear communication, and for creating a learning environment. While psychological safety is about feeling safe and secure, it does not happen at the expense of accountability or performance.

Matt Whiat explained how this paradox plays out at Barry-Wehmiller. "It sets such an extraordinarily high bar when you write a book titled *Everybody Matters*....I have to tell new employees, listen, it is still a J-O-B." During orientation, new hires are given a copy of Chapman's book and shown his TED Talk. Whiat said, initially, Chapman's concept can create thwarted expectations. "Suddenly, they're like, wait a second, this is a manufacturing job. This is rough."

While a workplace free of conflict may be pleasant, it is not necessarily psychologically safe. Have you ever heard an employee say, "I do not want to step on someone's toes, rock the boat, or ruffle feathers?" That is not psychological safety. Psychological safety emerges from a hard-earned harmony where people challenge each other to achieve collective goals. They are fully committed to a shared purpose. Accountability and constructive conflict become the standard.

As Chapman's servant leadership trickled down through his organization, employees found their passion, developed their skills, and shared their gifts. Barry-Wehmiller's recipe for organizational culture provides employees with a sense that their leaders authentically care. Employees feel supported, which allows them to risk vulnerability and contribute. In other words, Barry-Wehmiller has created a formula for a work culture containing the antecedent conditions necessary for psychological safety to emerge.

KEY CHAPTER TAKEAWAYS
- Prioritizing employees' well-being leads to better business outcomes.

- Engage the people closest to the problem by giving them the autonomy to solve it and get out of the way.
- When employees feel supported, it allows them to risk vulnerability and contribute.

CHAPTER 9:

WHAT WENT UP DIDN'T HAVE TO CRASH DOWN

"Success in an uncertain world depends on high-quality bets. High quality bets depend on high-quality conversations. These don't happen by accident."

—AMY EDMONDSON

In the Netflix documentary *Downfall: The Case Against Boeing*, there is an old aviation saying, "If it's not Boeing, I'm not going."[1] The adage speaks to the culture of excellence Boeing built and the trust it fostered with airlines, pilots, and the flying public. In five months, decades of goodwill evaporated after two passenger jets crashed, killing 346 people. This chapter explores Boeing leaders' role in the evolution of its culture, the sensemaking process, and the decisions made after the crashes. How much did Boeing's culture contribute to the disasters?

Boeing evolved in a low-competition environment, allowing engineers to focus on quality and safety. Excellence became Boeing's identity, the pillar of its work culture, and what earned public trust. From its 1916 founding until Airbus entered the scene in 1967, Boeing was the primary commercial airplane supplier in the world, and since the late 1960s, the Boeing 737 has dominated the market.

Airbus began as a multi-governmental effort by France, West Germany, and the United Kingdom. The fledgling consortium aimed to aggregate the European aerospace sector and provide a competitive alternative to Boeing. Lacking access to the US market, Airbus took off slowly. Nevertheless, Airbus continued to innovate and, in 1984, launched the affordable A320. Boeing, meanwhile, focused on the jumbo jet business and didn't modernize its offerings in the smaller plane market. For the first time, Boeing was facing fierce competition.

The rivalry intensified as the industry rapidly grew. US President Jimmy Carter signed the Airline Deregulation Act in October 1978. Suddenly, there was no longer a governor on competition. Free enterprise determined fares, routes, and market entry. Travel became more accessible with increased flights and decreased fares. Air passenger traffic exploded from eight hundred million passengers in 1980 to 4.6 billion just before the 2020 COVID-19 pandemic.[2]

In the 1990s, industry consolidation intensified competitive pressure again. Boeing gobbled up Rockwell International for more than three billion dollars in 1997, and it acquired its primary domestic rival, McDonnell Douglas, in a thirteen-billion-dollar stock swap the following year. Boeing needed the acquired manufacturing capacity to keep up with rising demand. A duopoly in the large jet market emerged between Boeing and Airbus.

The integration of McDonnell Douglas rocked Boeing. The new entity took Boeing's name, but as McDonnell Douglas executives ascended, Boeing's hallmark culture of quality and safety yielded to the pursuit of shareholder value.

The quality Boeing was once known for evaporated. "Before McDonnell Douglas, we just didn't take shortcuts because it just wasn't the Boeing culture," Cynthia Cole, a test and systems engineer and thirty-two-year Boeing veteran, said in the Netflix documentary. "You do it right, and you build in the quality and the safety, and the profits will follow. But all that changed, and it was just heartbreaking."[3]

In 2001, Boeing announced it would move its corporate offices from Seattle. "As we've grown, we have determined that our headquarters needs to be in a location central to all our operating units, customers and the financial community—but separate from our existing operations."[4] The last statement troubled Boeing employees. The Seattle team resented the demarcation line between the *suits and the boots*. It was a divorce, and management had custody of all the decisions without input about safety and quality from the people closest to the problems.

Harry Stonecipher gets much of the credit, or blame, for the changes to Boeing's culture. He was McDonnell Douglas's CEO, and after the merger, he served as president and COO from 1997 to 2002. Stonecipher acknowledged becoming a "lightning rod" for employee discontent because of his post-merger changes. "When people say I changed the culture of Boeing, that was the intent, so that it's run like a business rather than a great engineering firm."[5]

BOEING 737 MAX

Designing and manufacturing new airplanes is a high-risk proposition. Since its introduction in 1967. Boeing has chosen to revamp its proven 737 model rather than start from scratch.

Dennis Muilenburg, Boeing's CEO from 2015 to 2019, explained the risk/reward challenge of developing a new plane in the 2017 documentary *Airbus vs Boeing: The Jumbo Jet Race*. "Typically, the time from technology decision or launching a new airplane to the airplane being in the marketplace can be measured in five, ten years, perhaps more than a decade. And, typically, once those products are introduced, they will be in the hands of customers for decades to follow. We have a very long-cycle business, which means each decision we make is very important because it is a very capital-intensive business. It is very high investment upfront to create that future product because we have to get it right. We have to make the right bets, the right technology investment to reap decades of benefit."[6]

In December 2010, Airbus introduced the A320neo (new engine option), a more fuel-efficient direct competitor of Boeing's then-most recent iteration of its cash cow 737 NG (Next Generation). Boeing had been considering retiring its 737 lines for years but was caught flatfooted. It could not afford a potential decade of lead time to build a plane from scratch with the A32oneo already in production. Competition forced Boeing into another retooling of its existing product, and in August 2011, it announced the 737 MAX.

2018

Despite the MAX hype, Boeing employees' confidence in the plane had waned. In a February 8, 2018, exchange, an employee asked, "Would you put your family on a MAX simulator trained aircraft? I wouldn't."

"No," the coworker responded.

This exchange wasn't public knowledge then but came out during a later congressional investigation.[7]

Boeing seemed poised for growth. "By the beginning of 2018, we'd come through the safest period for commercial aviation in the history of aviation," *Wall Street Journal* reporter Andy Pasztor says in the Netflix documentary. "There actually hadn't been a big passenger jet crash anywhere in the world the previous year. Boeing has had so much success producing incredibly safe, reliable aircraft that pilots and passengers admired and loved to fly on. They had the public's trust. And then two planes dropped out of the sky."[8]

On October 29, 2018, Lion Air flight 610, a Boeing 737 MAX 8, crashed into the Java Sea shortly after takeoff, killing all 189 on board. Early in the investigation, Indonesia's National Transportation Safety Committee's suspected Boeing's anti-stall software—Maneuvering Characteristics Augmentation System (MCAS). The plane had issues on a flight the previous day. "In our view, the plane was not airworthy," an investigator said at a news conference in Jakarta.[9]

In November, the FAA issued an airworthiness directive for 737 MAX 8 and MAX 9, cautioning MCAS could make it difficult to control the plane due to repeated automated nose-down commands. Boeing said it was cooperating with investigators and evaluating the need for software or design changes, but it was confident in the safety features of the 737 MAX.

On November 13, Muilenburg went on Fox Business. "We've been very engaged with the investigative authorities throughout," he told host Maria Bartiromo. "The bottom line here is the 737 MAX is safe. Safety is a core value for us at Boeing."[10]

In December, an FAA internal report, Transport Airplane Risk Assessment Methodology (TARAM), cautioned that if Boeing did not fix the MCAS, there could be as many as fifteen additional crashes during the lifetime of the 737 MAX fleet if it were not grounded.[11]

On March 10, 2019, Ethiopian Airlines flight 302, a 737 MAX 8, crashed after takeoff from Addis Ababa, Ethiopia, killing all 157 onboard. The FAA completed the TARAM report four months before a second crash led to a global grounding of the MAX. Did the FAA and Boeing gamble with people's lives?

Shortly after the second crash, Congress began receiving information from whistleblowers and launched an investigation by the House Committee on Transportation and Infrastructure.[12]

It was becoming clear that Boeing took shortcuts in the rush to compete. The positioning of the MAX's new larger, more fuel-efficient engines changed the plane's aerodynamics. It led to instability and the potential for engine stalls when the aircraft was in a steep ascent. Boeing's solution was a software fix for a hardware problem. It failed to tell pilots about MCAS.[13] In April, Boeing admitted MCAS played a role in both crashes. The FAA and Boeing promised a thorough investigation.[14]

When Muilenburg appeared before the committee, Congressman DeFazio admonished him, "Wall Street, market forces, have a way of influencing the decisions of the best companies in the worst way, endangering the public and jeopardizing the good work of thousands of line workers. I hope that is not the story that will be written about this long-admired company."[15]

David Calhoun became Boeing's new CEO in 2020 after Muilenburg was fired. Calhoun took over amid a spectacle created when Boeing released hundreds of internal communications to Congress. The trove included this gem, "This airplane is designed by clowns, who in turn are supervised by monkeys." Rep. Peter DeFazio, D-Oregon, who was leading the MAX investigation, said the messages "paint a deeply disturbing picture of the lengths Boeing was apparently willing to go to in order to evade scrutiny from regulators, flight crews, and the flying public, even as its own employees were sounding alarms internally."[16]

TELL ME WHEN THE WHISTLE BLOWS

Ed Pierson, a senior manager at a Boeing factory, testified to the House committee that four months before the Lion Air crash, he emailed Scott Campbell, general manager of the 737 Max program. "Frankly right now all my internal warning bells are going off. And for the first time in my life, I'm sorry to say that I'm hesitant about putting my family on a Boeing airplane." He advocated for a production pause due to safety concerns related to schedule pressure and employee fatigue.[17]

In a 2021 interview, Pierson told Corporate Crime Reporter that he followed up his email to Campbell with a conversation.

"I told the boss—you have a dangerous, unstable production system, we need to shut down. We have to shut it down. He said to me—why do you feel that way? I gave him a list of examples. I told him—we need to shut down. He said—we can't shut down. I said—why not? I've seen people in the military shut down for lesser concerns. And that's when he came back and said—the military is not a profit making organization.

"I was so stunned by that. So this is a commercial operation and therefore it's okay to take chances with people's lives like that? It was also insulting to people in the military. It hit me—he's under a lot of pressure from Chicago."[18]

Two months after the Lion Air crash, Pierson wrote to the Boeing board of directors, the National Transportation Safety Board, and the Federal Aviation Administration. He eventually took his concerns to the press.

"I have no interest in scaring the public or wasting anyone's time," Pierson wrote the Boeing directors eighteen days before the Ethiopian Airlines crash. "I also don't want to wake up one morning and hear about another tragedy and have personal regrets."[19]

Boeing has maintained that it had no reason to believe that issues at the factory had played any role in the crashes. "Mr. Pierson raises issues about the production of the 737 MAX, yet none of the authorities investigating these accidents have found that production conditions in the 737-factory contributed in any way to these accidents."[20]

Pierson wasn't the only person sounding the alarm. After the Lion Air crash, FAA safety engineer Joe Jacobsen reviewed the black box data and quickly raised concerns about the MAX's safety. He noted insufficient sensor data was likely a culprit and was concerned that the airplane had been certified despite a deliberate design using a single sensor (Angle of Attack).

AoA sensors detect whether the wings have enough lift. Stalls can occur when the AoA reaches the critical point, and airflow becomes turbulent over the top of the wing. There was no redundancy for this flight-critical function. "I spoke to three managers with direct responsibility for this topic within the FAA. I told them that the use of one AoA input was a serious design flaw. All three were skeptical and already repeating the Boeing narrative... that the pilots should have been able to intervene," Jacobsen told one of the crash victim's family in a letter.[21]

LEADER SENSEMAKING

Imagine it is July 1, 2015. You are Dennis Muilenburg, and you have just been named Boeing CEO. You joined the company as an engineering intern in 1985 and have spent your entire thirty-year career at Boeing. You were part of the golden years of engineering and safety. You experienced firsthand the 1998 merger with McDonnell Douglas and the subsequent move of the corporate headquarters to Chicago—two events credited with wrecking Boeing's culture of excellence. As an engineer, you might even pine for the glory days.

As CEO, you have just put your hands on the yoke of a plane already in flight, and strong winds are influencing your course. It doesn't matter that when the decision was made to refurbish the 737 rather than retire it and build a plane from scratch, you led the company's Defense, Space, and Security division. Now, you are in control and starting to understand the multiple pressures CEOs face.

In addition to running the day-to-day, you also must serve as a navigator and decide where the ship is going. You face the internal pressure of being responsible for more than 140,000 people employed across the United States and in more than sixty-five countries.

You also have external expectations and burdens. It is out of your control that the government slashed the FAA's budget, and Boeing agreed to put some of its people in FAA oversight roles. Now, you are balancing a perverse relationship between submitting a product for approval and a Boeing engineer approving it as a quasi-FAA official.

Boeing investors expect shareholder value growth that commenced on Harry Stonecipher's cost-cutting watch to continue. Customers expect planes with lower operating costs and minimal training requirements, so they can pass the savings on to the flying public, which demands lower fares. Additionally, Boeing generates an estimated 1 percent of the United States' gross domestic product.[22] Your decisions could affect the broader economy.

Fast forward to the Lion Air flight crash. Engineers know the problem, and the fix is in development. Do you ground the plane and halt production?

Do not view this exercise as absolving Muilenburg or Boeing of any wrongdoing. It simply illustrates the mountain of decisions, pressures, and variables leaders weigh as they make sense of facts. Context and the business environment shape the decision-making process. Most of us have the luxury of going through our day without the demands executives face when it comes to sensemaking in a crisis. We have the luxury of limited choice—like a child coloring a kid's menu with a three-pack of crayons. Meanwhile, senior leaders are choosing from a 120-color box.

A religious podcast about integrating faith and work interviewed Muilenburg on October 3, 2018—just twenty-six days before the first MAX crash. He talked about adhering to the values of "hard work, integrity, respect for others, and how you treat people under pressure." He recalled these being standards he learned as a "farm kid" in Iowa. The interview took place days before a hurricane slammed the East Coast. He explained how Boeing evacuated a South Carolina production plant with about seven thousand employees. "For a time, we have to put our airplane production on hold and just take care of our people." Muilenburg then explained how one cannot separate the secular world from the private world, where you should keep your faith. "It has to be completely integrated. My faith is part of who I am."[23]

So why did Boeing seemingly make decisions that ran counter to ethical leadership? Why would Muilenburg, a man of deep faith, shut down for a hurricane but not advocate for shutting down the fleet until his team had resolved the maneuverability problem?

Comprehending the lessons of the Boeing crisis is a worthwhile exercise to show this type of failure is not solely the provenance of monsters or idiots. Decisions do not happen in a vacuum, and the powerful influence of external factors is a reality.

Boeing's leadership was responsible for stewarding its culture of excellence. Employees understood the potential consequences of their leaders' greedy decisions, but they could not stop "progress."

ETHICAL FADING

In 2000, during the merger with McDonnell Douglas, author Jim Collins, author of *Good to Great: Why Some Companies Make the Leap...And Others Don't* and *Built to*

Last: Successful Habits of Visionary Companies, shared his prescient concerns that the marriage would ultimately harm Boeing. "If in fact there's a reverse takeover, with the McDonnell ethos permeating Boeing, then Boeing is doomed to mediocrity. There's one thing that made Boeing really great all the way along. They always understood that they were an engineering-driven company, not a financially driven company. If they're no longer honoring that as their central mission, then over time they'll just become another company."[24]

The result of "just becoming another company" has been mediocrity, which has proven inadequate when people step onto your airplane and entrust you with their lives.

Ethical fading is a form of bias that is seldom premeditated and "occurs when people focus on some other aspect of a decision so that the ethical dimensions of the choice fade from view."[25] Blind spots can arise from information overload. Leaders must catch critical details in a sea of noise. Rationalizations, like Stonecipher's push to change Boeing's culture, can diminish unquantifiable value. Ego can play a role, too. Anyone who started as an intern in 1985 and experienced a near-vertical climb to the CEO could be presumptuous.

We likely will never know all the variables that Muilenburg faced or the pressures he felt as he made sense of Boeing's strategy for leading after the crisis. Did Boeing's lawyers tell him not to admit guilt and shift blame? Was he worried a shutdown could result in layoffs for some of his 140,000 employees? How much did the knowledge of the vast economic shadow cast by Boeing play into decisions?

Ethical fading is self-deception that allows us to behave in unethical ways while retaining the belief we are good people. "I've talked to high-level people inside Boeing who feel a sense of guilt, but they don't believe they did anything deliberately wrong," Dominic Gates, who won a Pulitzer Prize for coverage of the MAX, said in the documentary *Flight/Risk*. "The sin wasn't anything deliberate. It was going along with the system that was there and not questioning it enough. This is a very American story because it's the American corporate culture at the root of what's gone wrong."[26]

In October 2019, a few weeks before his termination, Muilenburg said, "It is critical we take a step back to humbly look at our culture."[27] He was right. The behaviors leaders exhibit and what behaviors they tolerate shape every organization's culture. In Boeing's case, an abrupt transition from a culture where engineers were critical collaborators in the mission to a cutthroat search for shareholder value ended in two preventable failures and the loss of 346 lives.

Boeing's website's Values page says, "In everything we do and in all aspects of our business, we will make safety our top priority, strive for first-time quality, hold ourselves to the highest ethical standards, and continue to support a sustainable future."[28] The MAX saga suggests a disconnect between Boeing's espoused and lived values.

Aviation analyst Michael Goldfarb spoke about the source of the gap, "Historically, Boeing was a culture of telling bad news. They discussed concerns freely in building planes. Now it became a problem that you do not bring bad news to the boss. Boeing had highly paid CEOs, whose main incentive was to increase the stock price and to please Wall Street. These CEOs demanded that all their managers hit their marks, and they don't care how they do that."[29] Focusing solely on profit and inhibiting employee voice extinguishes psychological safety and runs counter to living a mission of safety and quality.

People make sense of their environment by watching and listening to how leaders live out their values. Ben Horowitz suggests, "A person may come in with high integrity but have to compromise it to succeed in your environment. People become the culture they live in and do what they have to do to survive and thrive."[30] It appears Horowitz's statement may apply to leaders, too.

KEY CHAPTER TAKEAWAYS

- Leaders weigh a mountain of decisions, pressures, and variables as they make sense of facts, creating information overload, which can cause blind spots.
- Ethical fading occurs when people prioritize other factors over the moral dimensions of a decision.
- A work culture will support or compromise ethical decision-making based on what a leader tolerates.

CHAPTER 10:

CAN YOU HEAR ME NOW?

"The great enemy of communication, we find, is the illusion of it."

—WILLIAM WHYTE

Dad and I always struggled with communication. Before the hospital expanded to twenty-four-hour service, the doctors rotated on-call coverage after-hours for clients with emergencies. Evidently, as a three-year-old, I took exception to this. I must have sensed something when Dad shifted into professional mode. Maybe his tone changed. Perhaps I just needed his full attention after not seeing him all day. As soon as he picked up the phone and started talking to a client, I would transform into something resembling a soccer hooligan ringing a cowbell.

We took a family trip to Wisconsin to visit one of Dad's vet school classmates. Dad shared his telephone troubles. His friend, Tom, had two young children and a perfect solution—P.E.T. It had worked wonders with his girls. This book, *Parent Effectiveness Training: The "No-Lose" Program for Raising Responsible Children*, was a panacea.[1]

Dad was stoked to give it a try. Back home, he sat me on his knee and provided frank, constructive criticism. P.E.T. suggested we have an intellectual discussion and arrive at a mutually beneficial solution. Dad said there was a fog as I pondered his question about my distracting behavior. Then as I looked around the room, he saw my face light up. I turned to him lovingly, saying, "Why don't you take that gum over there and stick it up your nose."

Dad elected to leave the old, chewed gum in the ashtray. He tossed the P.E.T. book in the trash and called Tom to thank him for the sage advice. The moment foreshadowed our communication for the next forty-plus years.

The analogy is more than an amusing parenting fail. It is a lesson about why communication is so hard. Employees seldom have enough knowledge or a vantage point to see the big picture and develop a shared understanding with their leader. However, as leaders, we grasp our intended communication completely. While employees certainly have more awareness and capacity than a three-year-old, they, too, struggle with sensemaking when information is ambiguous or incomplete.

VITAL COMMUNICATION

As we saw in chapter 5, our mind is not a tabula rasa. Communication is filtered both in delivery and on receipt by our lived experiences. "When another person speaks, you hear both less and more than they mean. *Less* because none of us can express the full extent of our understanding, and *more* because what another says is constantly mixing and interacting with your own knowledge and puzzlements," according to Richard Rumelt.[2]

Additionally, the receiver must account for voids. Leaders do not just omit facts; emotional and symbolic gaps exist. As employees make sense of the unknown, their brains fill in these gaps. Thinking their message is wholly communicated, leaders can function in different realities than employees. This disconnect can result in confusion, ambiguity, anxiety, and hampered performance.

Our inherent defenses make all feedback seem personal. If leaders are not careful, employees will internalize feedback, not as constructive advice about how they can succeed. Instead, they will hear how they have failed— not just in their work but as a human being. Leaders can mitigate communication failures with clarity, consistency, and transparency. Researchers described transparency as a function of how leaders interact and share information. They suggested leaders must also be clear about why they made decisions and be open to receiving feedback.[3]

I attended dozens of pre-shift communication meetings during my research in the distribution center. Negativity and ambiguity were typical. In nearly every meeting, I heard supervisors threatening employees: "If you don't (wear your seat belt...go to break on time...fill out forklift inspection sheets...etc.), I'm writing you up."

In one meeting, a supervisor announced a new policy for pedestrian traffic. The old walkway funneled people through high-danger areas where trucks were being loaded and unloaded. However, the supervisor failed to explain why management was rerouting employees. All they heard was a significantly longer walk to the time clock. When asked if additional grace time would be allowed so they were not considered late, they were told no. As frustration rose, the employees and supervisor began shouting. The meeting ended abruptly when the supervisor yelled, "If you don't like it, go see HR," and then he retreated to his office.

Shifts started in two waves. I sensed déjà vu an hour and a half later when the second group began assembling at the office. Before this meeting became contentious, an operator asked, "Are they changing the walkway for safety reasons?" The employees accepted the new policy without further debate because of one straightforward question.

Despite cryptic, vague, and threatening messages being what the operators were accustomed to, many employees heralded a new supervisor for his communication. He focused start-up meetings on setting expectations and helping his team understand the business. This supervisor was transparent about the workload and shared information about planned versus actual schedule progress. He also explained how the volume might impact them in the coming days.

"The morning meeting used to be just the most negative thing ever," one of his reports told me. "But now, I think the people on the floor feel better about the work they're doing because they know it's actually gonna make a difference." Employees soon began considering the link between their individual performance and group outcomes like mandatory overtime.

EMPLOYEE VOICE BEHAVIOR

The Five Dysfunctions of a Team: A Leadership Fable by Patrick Lencioni theorizes that differences of opinion are an attempt to find the best possible solution in the shortest amount of time. When done respectfully between employees, conflict improves productivity.[4]

Employee voice behavior is critical for maintaining a healthy work culture. These behaviors foster innovation and collaboration and encourage proactive rather than reactive problem-solving. An organization that promotes dialogue with its employees will tend to be more adaptable, resilient, and successful. Teams are more effective when they get input from all members, and psychological safety becomes evident when the team welcomes ideas from people at the margins.[5]

Taken out of context, a leader can perceive simple acts like being approached for help or suggesting a change as challenging authority.[6] Researchers define employee voice behavior as a constructive challenge.[7] They suggest that when employees consciously choose to speak up, it is beyond defined job obligations and should viewed as a positive voice rather than a dissenting one.[8] They advise leaders to recognize differing opinions and resistance as a counteroffer, not a challenge, and that a subordinate's pushback is often a symptom of being in an information vacuum.[9]

STIFLING VOICE

When I was managing the veterinary clinic, we held a staff training meeting about our migration to electronic medical records. I had recently returned from a seminar where I learned the average full-time veterinarian misses or gives away $98,450 in revenue annually, and our hospital had twelve veterinarians. The owners had been very transparent with the business financials and explained the impact of the missed charges. For weeks, we had been training on new system-driven protocols that would help mitigate much of the risk of missing charges and lost revenue.

Toward the end of a meeting, a long-tenured employee went off script and asked, "Why can't we get a raise?" The staff was irritated because the owners had just purchased some property adjacent to the clinic. They wanted the organization to give out raises, not make a real estate investment.

The owners had not stolen a wheelbarrow full of money from the payroll safe to purchase the building. A separate Limited Liability Company owned the organization's properties, which was unknown to the employees.

Everyone was frustrated. The staff wanted a raise, wanted better benefits, and wanted more paid time off, yet they were unwilling to follow new protocols designed to mitigate missed charges and increase revenue. Dad shut down the meeting by saying, "Ask the client for a raise," and walked out. We lost an opportunity to educate and advocate. We did not explain *the why*.

Even when leaders exhibit supportive behaviors, employees' use of their voice is tenuous. "One of the most fundamental challenges organizations face is how to manage the interpersonal threats inherent in employees admitting ignorance or uncertainty, voicing concerns and opinions, or simply being different," according to Edmondson.[10] There are many reasons to encourage employees to be vulnerable and speak up. Perhaps the best reason is to eliminate preventable failures.

PREVENTABLE FAILURE

STS-51-L, the twenty-fifth mission of NASA's Space Shuttle program, epitomizes an avoidable failure. Engineers had identified a quality control problem months before and warned that something could go terribly wrong. Managers repeatedly rebuffed the engineers for providing inconclusive data to support their concerns. Communication was mired in bureaucracy, making it difficult for minority or dissenting views to rise through the organizational hierarchy.

The Space Shuttle Challenger's tenth mission and final flight occurred on January 28, 1986.

The night before the launch, executives from NASA contractor Morton Thiokol, a contingent of Morton Thiokol engineers, and NASA were on a six-hour conference call debating the viability of Challenger's launch the following day. The engineers wanted to postpone the launch, fearing that the company's O-rings would malfunction due to the cold temperature. Their apprehension grew when the thermometer in Florida plunged below freezing. Morton Thiokol's vice president of engineering, Bob Lund, supported the engineers' recommendation to postpone the launch.[11]

NASA officials on the call challenged the advice. The shuttle program managers were desperate to prove they could launch reliably. STS-51-L had already been pushed back twice. NASA's George Hardy said, "I am appalled by your recommendation."[12]

Another shuttle program manager, Lawrence Mulloy, added, "My God, Thiokol, when do you want me to launch—next April?"[13]

Morton Thiokol's senior vice president Jerry Mason turned to Lund and suggested he "take off his engineering hat and put on his management hat."[14]

Shortly after, Morton Thiokol's managers voted unanimously to recommend Challenger's launch. They reasoned that their data was inconclusive while the frigid weather conditions remained a concern.[15]

Roger Boisjoly, a booster rocket engineer who had been on the call debating whether to launch Challenger, said, "I never [would] take [away] any management right to take the input of an engineer and then make a decision based upon that input, and I truly believe that....I personally felt that management was under a lot of pressure to launch and that they made a very tough decision, but I didn't agree with it."[16]

None of the engineers did, nor did they participate in drafting the new recommendation to launch. The executive managers were the only ones to sign the document. Boisjoly said, "I was not even asked to participate in giving any input to the final decision charts."[17]

At launch, Boisjoly and a colleague sat in a Morton Thiokol conference room. They were certain if there were problems, it would happen at takeoff. An O-ring seal did fail, but aluminum oxides quickly resealed the hole before any flames could escape and cause an explosion. As the shuttle cleared the tower, relief started to creep in.

"Thirteen seconds later, we saw it blow up," Boisjoly said.[18]

Wind shear had reopened the wound, resulting in the Challenger breaking up over the Atlantic Ocean seventy-three seconds after launch.[19] Astronauts Dick Scobee, Mike Smith, Ellison Onizuka, Judy Resnik, Ron McNair, Greg Jarvis, and a schoolteacher, Christa McAuliffe, who was to be the first civilian into space, were all killed.[20]

Six months before the launch, Boisjoly sent a memo regarding the failure of Morton Thiokol's seals in cold temperatures based on his inspections from previous missions. "The result would be a catastrophe of the highest order—loss of human life," he forewarned.[21]

In June of 1986, President Reagan formed the Rogers Commission panel, headed by former Secretary of State William P. Rogers, to investigate the incident. The commission's findings were that the O-ring design flaw was the root cause of the accident, but they were critical of the communication leading to the launch decision.[22]

Years after the disaster, Allan McDonald, Morton Thiokol's lead engineer on the project, reflected on his decision not to sign the launch recommendation and emphasized the importance of psychological safety. "In my entire career, I've never, ever heard a dumb question," he said. "I've heard a lot of dumb answers."[23]

There are alarming similarities between the NASA and Boeing tragedies regarding preventable failures. In both cases, leaders rushed decisions due to external pressure. NASA felt it had to prove it could reliably launch after multiple delays. Boeing was facing competitive pressure.

Like the NASA engineers' efforts to stop the Challenger launch, whistleblowers had warned about the 737 MAX's potential for tragedy. Both organizations restricted or inhibited the critical bottom-up flow of information. People who anticipated the tragedies could not navigate hierarchy and bureaucracy to prevent disasters.

DEFENSIVE SILENCE

I would argue the root cause of the Boeing crashes began well before MCAS became a Band-Aid software solution for the 737 MAX's hardware design flaw. It can be traced back to Boeing's culture change. Unlike Stonecipher's approach of shutting down dialogue, the goal of communication in every healthy relationship should be to have two-way communication.

Without psychological safety, organizational communication risks becoming a monologue, or what researchers have identified as defensive silence.[24] We are hardwired only to touch a hot stove once. We learn to fear the burn. Continual rebukes and being "shut down" by a boss can lead to employees abandoning communication. Employees may get in such a rut that they forget contributing is an option.[25]

Conservation of resources theory suggests employees adopt avoidant or passive tactics to preserve limited resources and mitigate psychological discomfort.[26] This silence, an intentionally counterproductive work behavior, impedes individual and organizational performance.[27] When emotionally exhausted people disengage, it has a detrimental effect on morale and harms the work culture.[28]

"We were talking to the right people," Boisjoly said. "We were talking to the people who had the power to stop that launch."[29] He explained why he stopped disputing at the Challenger prelaunch meeting with NASA. "There was no point in me doing anything any further than I had already attempted to do...[but] I left the room feeling badly defeated."[30]

This example of failed communication should be a lesson for leaders because preventable failures are seldom identified and handed to you on a platter. Without psychological safety and two-way communication, a crisis may be the first time you learn of a problem.

PROMOTING EMPLOYEE VOICE

Even when leaders are supportive, getting employees to speak up is tenuous. Unfortunately, not everyone has the freedom to speak candidly. "Giving a voice to all people is the foundation of an organization that is willing to experiment and learn," according to management consultants Heifetz and Laurie. "But, in fact, whistleblowers, creative deviants, and other such original voices routinely get smashed and silenced in organizational life."[31]

With inclusive behaviors, leaders can minimize headwinds for upward communication and overcome the power dynamics of organizational hierarchy. Research has shown that management openness is the most influential leadership behavior in promoting employee voice. It suggests leaders are vital to removing barriers because speaking up is a discretionary effort, and employees who contribute can be viewed as provocative.[32] Leaders can promote employee voice by guaranteeing courageous individuals who risk vulnerability will not face negative consequences.

A counterintuitive approach to inclusion is to create a formal space for dissenters. The legacy employee at the animal hospital who derailed the staff meeting with a question about a raise became an ally. When I promoted them to the leadership team, everyone thought I was crazy. Critics are often the people who have the greatest need for inclusion. Knowledge is power, and access to it can help people develop an enterprise mindset. When that happens, your antagonists can become your advocates. At a minimum, if you give them a voice, they will always be there to play devil's advocate, challenge ideas, prevent groupthink, and help you make informed decisions.

Inclusion does not have to be as risky as promoting a disgruntled employee. Sometimes, simply taking a people-centric approach can increase engagement and encourage employee voice behaviors. During my research, communication between managers and employees in the distribution center was minimal and predominantly negative.

"If someone was a rockstar employee, we were leaving them alone, so really, the only reason supervisors were going to someone was because they did something wrong," the HR coordinator told me early in my research. "I can't tell you the last time I heard about someone going up to an employee and saying, 'So, hey, what's going on?' Or, 'How's your kids?'"

When Jose arrived, everything changed. "When people listen, it makes you want to do your job better because they take an interest in you as an individual," a forklift operator explained.

Inclusive leader behaviors can stimulate two-way communication. Psychological safety mediates the relationship between a leader's behavior and the employee's decision to contribute their thoughts or remain silent.[33] In other words, leader behavior is like turning a knob on the stove. Psychological safety is the heat that makes the water boil. Feeling psychologically safe allows employees to risk vulnerability and information to bubble up.

KEY CHAPTER TAKEAWAYS
- Employees seldom have enough knowledge or a vantage point to see the big picture and develop a shared understanding with their leader.
- Our lived experiences act as a filter and can obscure communication.
- Leaders should recognize differing opinions and resistance as a counteroffer, not a challenge.
- Teams are more effective when they get input from all members, and psychological safety is evident when the team welcomes people's ideas at the margins.
- Leaders can promote employee voice by guaranteeing courageous individuals who risk vulnerability will not face negative consequences.

CHAPTER 11:

FOSTERING PSYCHOLOGICAL SAFETY

"In general, the route to establishing psychological safety begins with the team's leader. So if you are leading a team—be it a group of coworkers or a sports team, a church gathering, or your family dinner table—think about what message your choices send."

—CHARLES DUHIGG

Upon completing my doctoral program, I joined BEATTY Leadership in St. Louis, Missouri, under the guidance of my friend and mentor, Dr. Ann Beatty. A distinguished industrial-organizational psychologist, Dr. Beatty's expertise in C-suite coaching, executive assessment, and succession planning has benefitted some of the world's most successful companies.

I was in awe of Dr. Beatty's bespoke process for vetting people and understanding what makes them tick. She utilizes hundreds of data points to project a candidate's fit for a prospective role. The evaluation includes a prospect's stress tolerance, emotional self-awareness, learning orientation, intellectual horsepower, and other traits. We helped organizations avoid costly talent mistakes and helped people recognize, understand, and act on their "developmental imperatives."

Fresh off three years of intense research, I kept looking for ways to interject psychological safety into our work. Dr. Beatty was very patient, but at one point, she suggested I would eventually learn to use all the tools at my disposal as my coaching and consulting career evolved.

It was the Maslow talk: "If all you have is a hammer, everything looks like a nail."

It was not an admonishment; it was sage advice.

Looking back, it's clear that Dr. Beatty and I approached leadership from different angles. She focused on finding a fit for the client's existing context or a solution for a specific problem. On the other hand, I was grappling with a fundamental question: Is leadership about finding the right people for an environment, or can a psychologically safe culture create a diverse, inclusive place where no wrong people exist? We were operating at different levels of abstraction. I was playing checkers; Dr. Beatty was playing chess. In the end, she was right. Our clients hired us to assess their candidates or problems, not their culture or leadership effectiveness.

I have discussed how positive leader behaviors are catalysts for psychological safety to emerge. Through sensemaking, the collective perceptions of the leader and the environment begin to form the work culture. An organization's work culture moderates the relationship between psychological safety and performance. In other words, a positive or negative work culture represents a team's level of psychological safety, which functions like a valve that enables or restricts productivity. For this reason, while individuals experience psychological safety, it is most impactful when it aggregates in a team, and everyone supports a common goal.

The balance of this chapter discusses a leadership model that aligns individuals with an organization's purpose and fosters a culture where psychological safety can emerge and scale across teams.

PURPOSE

Shared purpose can build individual hardiness and organizational resilience. If an organization's mission is *what* it does, and leadership is *how* it realizes the mission, the purpose is *why* an organization exists.

I've encountered many leaders who question the value and relevance of theoretical and strategic discussions about mission, vision, values, and purpose. One former boss described it as "mental masturbation," and a decade ago, I agreed with him.

During my over twenty years in logistics, shipping and delivering people's household basics and material things seldom provided a sense of deep purpose. Mostly, I loathed what I did. It was a job. I remember my dad talking about how blessed he felt to be a veterinarian: "I love what I do. It isn't work."

Occasionally, I would get a taste of purpose. As a UPS driver, I delivered packages late on Christmas Eve. Most people had given up hope that the gifts in my truck would find their way under the tree for Christmas morning. Santa is real, and his job is magical. People's gratitude filled me with pride as I handed off the Christmas morning saving presents. Unfortunately, the experience was fleeting.

Years later, I was a weekend manager in a Walgreens distribution center. I recall having a deep sense of purpose when we rushed truckloads of bottled water and batteries to Florida after Hurricane Ike. Nearly every other weekend, missing family time trumped making sure people had their sundries and As Seen on TV gadgets.

In many places I have worked, even if I had known the organization's aspirational "whys," any sense of purpose would have been hollow. Actions spoke louder than words, and the primacy of shareholder value was unmistakable.

The cadence of reporting earnings disrupted employees' lives at one career stop. For the last two weeks of every quarter, no one was allowed to take vacation or use PTO. We pulled orders scheduled for the subsequent quarter to inflate the current quarter's earnings. The consumer demand for the merchandise was unconnected. All that mattered was the bill of sale attesting to the purchase. These rush orders often sat for days or weeks before carriers picked them up. Workers put birthdays and anniversary celebrations on hold. They missed graduations, basketball games, and dance recitals.

Greed punished the workforce every quarter. We robbed Peter to pay Paul, ensuring the process would repeat in thirteen weeks.

For purpose to be activated to help an organization achieve its potential, it must be authentic, resonate with employees, and be about more than generating economic value. Employees quickly sniff out hypocrisy, insincerity, and platitudes. Without a strong sense of purpose, it is human nature to fall into a rut performing the mundane routine tasks that make up our jobs.

A consulting colleague shared a conversation they had with a frustrated utilities executive. It illustrates that it is hard to be "on" all the time. The leader said, "What we need is a really good storm." When the stakes are high, purpose is palpable.

Inspiring the veterinary hospital staff to do the right thing every time was hard. Cleaning up vomit and diarrhea isn't quite as sexy as administering lifesaving CPR and assisting with delivering puppies. Still, these tasks are vital to disease control and prevention.

A doorbell rang in the clinic's ICU when someone arrived with an emergency. In that instant—a really good storm—the organization shifted gears. Our staff was at its best when our clients and patients were at their worst. It is awe-inspiring to watch a veterinary team in action. Veterinary doctors, technicians, and staff are real-life superheroes. Everyone had a role. The staff who were not saving lives were comforting clients.

Developing cultures where a sense of purpose has seeped into the collective consciousness is easier in roles like healthcare, where altruism is an intrinsic motivator. Research shows nine out of ten people are willing to earn less money to do meaningful work.[1] However, we saw in chapter 8 that leveraging purpose can happen in any environment. CEO Bob Chapman shifted manufacturing company Barry-Wehmiller's focus from stakeholder capitalism to shareholder capitalism by using *The Extraordinary Power of Caring for Your People Like Family*, the subtitle of his book *Everybody Matters*.

OVERCOMING THE IMPEDIMENT

Work culture stands between business strategy and business success. How can you lead an organization to reach its potential when talent optimization and culture change are so enigmatic? Everyone is looking for a quick fix, three easy steps, or a top ten hacks for fixing their work culture.

The model below is based on my doctoral research. Its components represent antecedent conditions required for psychological safety to emerge. It is not a step-by-step sequential model. Instead, it is a diagnostic tool for framing work culture and identifying the origins and impact of organizational friction and competing values.

The fostering psychological safety model is a feedback loop that functions like Jim Collins's Flywheel Effect, which he uses to illustrate how momentum builds during change. Collins describes this process as "relentlessly pushing a giant, heavy flywheel, turn upon turn, building momentum until a point of breakthrough, and beyond." Like change momentum, as psychological safety propagates, "You're pushing no harder than during the first rotation, but the flywheel goes faster and faster. Each turn of the flywheel builds upon work done earlier, compounding your investment of effort," Collins explained in *Good to Great*.[2]

Like the Flywheel Effect, psychologically safe cultures build momentum and reinforce themselves over time. This model is a strategy for merging leadership and purpose to help an organization achieve its potential. Strong relationships and supportive, affirming leader behaviors make the culture and the employees more resilient. The team will begin to shun behaviors that distract it from achieving shared goals. No model can be all-encompassing, but embedded in this loop is most organizational friction detrimental to work culture, employee well-being, and achieving business results. The key elements are:

#1 **Ethical Leadership**: Integrity is having the moral courage to do the right thing every time. A collapse of integrity typically precedes ethical failures.

Imagine how whistleblower Frances Haugen felt knowing that Facebook was concealing internal research about the negative impact of Instagram on teen girls' mental health. She was dismayed that its "engagement-based ranking" exposed teens to unhealthy corners of the internet. "I'm here today because I believe Facebook's products harm children, stoke division, and weaken our democracy," Haugen said in her 2021 testimony before Congress. "The company's leadership knows ways to make Facebook and Instagram safer but won't make the necessary changes because they have put their immense profits before people."[3]

Hagen went on to list multiple examples of ethical breakdowns and ultimately proclaimed Facebook should declare "moral bankruptcy" and compared it to the likes of companies selling tobacco and opioids.

A case study from the University of Texas explains the role of self-serving bias, the tendency to consider information in ways that serve an individual's self-interest, played at Facebook. "If you happened to own a big chunk of Facebook shares, as most of the company's 'deciders' no doubt do, decisions that help the firm's profitability and stock price performance might well seem to be the right thing to do even though they're just the right thing for them."[4]

Because people tend to mirror their leaders' behaviors and values, leadership must begin with integrity and modeling ethical behaviors.

#2 **Candor and Accountability**: Leaders need to be candid, consistent, and just. They can only hold subordinates accountable for things they understand and control. When people fall short, they must understand how their behavior negatively affects outcomes. It needs to be a learning opportunity tied to the organization's purpose.

Too often, timid leaders fail employees and sidestep these difficult conversations. They avoid conflict in the name of harmony, but candor is an act of respect. It gives struggling people a chance for redemption. "When bosses are too invested in everyone getting along, they also fail to encourage the people on their team to criticize one another for fear of sowing discord,"

Kim Malone Scott explains. "They create the kind of work environment where being 'nice' is prioritized at the expense of critiquing and therefore improving actual performance."[5]

In 2013, the Chief of the Australian Army, Lieutenant General David Morrison, faced a sex scandal resulting from subordinates' unacceptable behavior that degraded and objectified women. Morrison was unambiguous in his response. "Those who think that it is okay to behave in a way that demeans or exploits their colleagues have no place in this army," he said. "If that doesn't suit you, get out." He vowed to be "ruthless in ridding the army of people who cannot live up to its values."[6]

Morrison encouraged everyone to take a stand against unacceptable behavior. He then explained how avoidance is a leadership failure. "The standard you walk past is the standard you accept." Ultimately, more than 170 soldiers were terminated or disciplined for distributing explicit emails.[7]

When candor and accountability are lacking, it is harmful not only to those involved, but it also creates a sense of injustice among the rest of the team and distracts the organization from its purpose and executing its mission.

#3 **Words and Deeds**: Leaders must remember they are always on stage, and their intent does not matter, but their words and deeds do. Employees scrutinize them as part of the individual and collective sensemaking processes. Remember my communication gaffe from chapter 7 when I told the veterinary clinic employees that they were the organization's fourth priority? Or when my dad abruptly ended a meeting by walking out in frustration and suggesting the staff should "ask the client for a raise" in chapter 9? In both cases, we intended to communicate that *if there is no margin, there can be no mission*; however, if we can make the business healthy, there will be more resources for raises and benefits.

We failed miserably. Our message and our actions were misaligned. The employees did not have a chance to make sense of our communication.

Fortunately, we weren't always that bad at communicating, and we learned to recognize and reward constructive conflict. One communication success story I'd encourage leaders to replicate is what Dad did in his medical director role. Monthly, he met with each veterinarian for a level-set meeting. The agenda was always the same two questions:

- What do you want to be when you grow up?
- What is one thing you'd change about the clinic?

The boundaries of their job description, department, or even current employer did not constrain the veterinarians' answers. In asking question one, he often learned about the person, not just the employee. He knew about people's passions and aspirations within veterinary medicine and beyond. Answers led to opportunities for continuing education and advanced certification. We had doctors develop specializations in

Chinese Medicine, acupuncture, critical care, advanced ultrasound, hospice, and end-of-life care. It allowed the organization to expand services, but more importantly, it fostered the veterinarians' sense of collegiality.

In asking question two, people had a place to vent about policies and procedures that negatively affected their jobs, clients, or patients. It allowed doctors to feel heard, let the enterprise explain its perspective, and created a punch list of things to fix.

These monthly meetings built trust and bolstered collective purpose.

#4 **Trustworthiness:** In the April 2021 issue of *The Army Resilience Directorate Newsletter,* Major Kimberly Brutsche and Captain Tiarra McDaniel published an article on psychological safety. The authors, who served at West Point's Simon Center for the Professional Military Ethic, juxtaposed two types of personal courage they witnessed in the army. One is ingrained in the culture, and one needs to be. "Courage is frequently correlated to fearless acts of great honor on the battlefield, but seldomly to actions in garrison."[8]

Their piece challenges leaders to get comfortable with the uncomfortable and disavow the stigma associated with ordinary life problems. They highlight the tension between a masculine military culture and help-seeking behaviors. They ask how battlefield bravery can be replicated in daily life to support the well-being of their fellow soldiers.[9]

Soldiers are people, too. They face the same obstacles as civilians: discrimination, sexual assault, addiction, mental illness, and failure. Like all humans, admitting fallibility comes with fear of being ostracized. "It is dangerous for leaders to perpetuate this mindset in our military culture because we then leave our Soldiers to fight alone, just as if we left them on the battlefield," the authors said. The concern is more acute in a Machismo culture where having a problem is stigmatized as a weakness. The authors correctly assert, "To create the psychological safety necessary for Soldiers to be courageous daily, leaders must create an inclusive culture built on trust."[10]

The conundrum of leaders fostering an environment where people dare to seek help is an excellent example of the relationship between trust and psychological safety. Leaders can promote trust through relationships. If you are authentic and caring, employees may deem you trustworthy and give you the benefit of the doubt. As you develop meaningful relationships where employees feel psychologically safe, they trust you will extend them the same courtesy. It frees employees to be vulnerable, ask for help, share their opinions, or admit failure.

#5 **Relational Leadership**: Leadership is a process that develops from people's interactions; it is not a trait of the person in charge. Leaders garner influence through building and nurturing these relationships. Research shows that the leader's task-focused behaviors directly impact firm performance. Their relationship-focused behaviors affect employees' attitudes and well-being, indirectly impacting performance.[11] Leaders must leverage both tools to optimize talent and foster a healthy culture.

In chapter 6, when the facility manager threw an unsanctioned Super Bowl party for a group of cynical, weary forklift operators, he had to weigh being a good steward of the facility budget and the customer's supply chain with empathy for his employees. He was balancing his task and relational skills. The corporate HR director told me, "The fact that he had enough respect for their time and participated in it is exactly what they appreciated."

This behavioral complexity distinguishes managers from leaders. "You manage things; you lead people," Rear Admiral Grace Murray Hopper said. Adeptness with task- and relationship-focused behaviors allows leaders to engage all stakeholders, regardless of their position in the organizational hierarchy.[12]

#6 Perceived Organizational Support: As employees make sense of how much the organization "values their contributions and cares about their well-being," it profoundly affects their outlook and behaviors. Employees make sense of feeling supported through tangible benefits like competitive compensation and intangible support like autonomy, freedom of creativity, and feeling like they have an opportunity for growth.[13]

Perceiving support is paramount to creating a climate that promotes psychological safety. In the presence of support, employees are more likely to exhibit voice behaviors and feel compelled to contribute by speaking their minds.[14] In contrast, when employees do not feel supported, perceptions of psychological safety diminish, and vital two-way communication fades.[15]

#7 **Values Alignment**: Values are a fundamental component of an organization's culture. "Empty values statements create cynical and dispirited employees, alienate customers, and undermine managerial credibility," Patrick Lencioni states.[16] However, when a person's values mirror and intertwine with their employer's values, it contributes to a synergy due to the natural fit. This alignment helps employees feel connected to the organization's purpose and satisfied in their work. Ultimately, shared values foster a positive culture and boost performance, which lead to better teamwork, collaboration, and communication.

In 2023, Patagonia, an outdoor clothing company, shared its updated its values on X. "For our fiftieth year, we're looking forward, not back, to life on Earth. Together, we can prioritize purpose over profit...and protect this wondrous planet, our only home."[17] The message resonates with consumers. The company ranked first in an Axios-Harris poll on the one hundred most reputable US companies in 2023.[18]

Patagonia integrates its core beliefs and values of quality, integrity, environmentalism, justice, and not being bound by convention into its supply chain.[19] It works closely with manufacturers to ensure they produce products that align with its values.

Actions like that are not atypical, but some other ways Patagonia walks its talk are genuinely distinctive. In 2011, Patagonia ran a full-page Black Friday advertisement in the *New York Times* about its top-selling R2 fleece. It read, "Don't Buy This Jacket." The ad explained the jacket's manufacturing process and urged consumers to consider the environmental impact of producing the garment before purchasing.[20]

The company intentionally hires employees who share its values. It encourages workers to participate in peaceful environmental protests. If an employee gets arrested for protesting, Patagonia pays their bail and legal fees and compensates them for missed work time.

In 2022, Patagonia's founder, Yvon Chouinard, bequeathed the company and its estimated one-hundred-million-dollar annual profit to a charity that combats climate change.[21]

What does this do for employee engagement, their understanding of their place in the company, and how they contribute to Patagonia's purpose? Measuring it is difficult, but one metric suggests that value alignment is a powerful motivator. Patagonia's employee turnover rate is 4 percent.[22] In the US, the average rate is 17.3 percent.[23]

#8 Inclusion and Belonging: The owner of DEI consulting firm Equision, Dr. Salwa Rahim-Dillard, told me, "Inclusion is the perception and feeling of belonging and being valued for the full authentic expression of your culture and self."

Creating an environment where genuine people can be present is empowering and inspiring. Sociologist Martha Beck describes the feeling. "When you experience unity of intention, fascination, and purpose, you live like a bloodhound on a scent, joyfully doing what feels truest in each moment."[24]

Actualizing inclusion eliminates the need for people to wear inauthentic masks and change their persona to meet some others' expectations of their experience in the role. When leaders fail to foster an inclusive culture, it creates a decision point that shifts the burden of participation and engagement to the out-group. "Instead of making authentic choices, we make choices based on the part we're playing," Will Marré explains. "Our lives are dictated, to a large degree, by what we think we must do to remain members in good standing of whatever club we have decided to join."[25] Inclusive leadership can mitigate this burden placed on new and marginalized employees.

The Society for Human Resource Management defines belonging as "having that same feeling at work as you do in a personal setting with friends where you feel comfortable to be there, to share your opinions, to feel truly cared about and accepted, and not afraid to be yourself. You belong."[26] How people make sense of belonging relates to many personal characteristics like racial and gender representation, sexual orientation, disability, or physical appearance. Leaders play critical roles in creating an accepting culture where employees feel like they belong because culture is defined by what leaders tolerate. Are your employees, and more importantly, your leaders, supportive of those on your organization's periphery?

#9 Courage: In this model, courage brackets psychological safety. It takes courage to raise your hand, share an opinion, or question authority—to risk being vulnerable. For leaders, the strategic awareness and courage to swallow pride and respond productively to acts of vulnerability is vital. "The true test is how leaders respond when people actually do speak up," Edmondson says in her book, *The Fearless Organization.* "If a boss responds with anger or disdain as soon as someone steps forward to speak up about a problem, the safety will quickly evaporate."[27]

Psychological safety only stands a chance with leaders exhibiting supportive behaviors, personal humility, and measured responses. However, when leaders are courageous, the psychological safety flywheel "builds momentum" and "goes faster and faster," creating a resilient, engaged, high-performing culture.

KEY CHAPTER TAKEAWAYS
- Positive leader behaviors are a catalyst for psychological safety to emerge.
- Through sensemaking, the collective perceptions of the leader and the environment begin to form the work culture.
- Understanding the shared purpose—a company's reason for existing—can build individual hardiness and organizational resilience.

- For a purpose to resonate with employees and be activated, it needs to be about more than generating economic value.

- The repetition of positive sensemaking is critical for the culture change process and how leaders can ensure the new culture takes root.

CHAPTER 12:

BUZZING THE TOWER

"To handle yourself, use your head; to handle others, use your heart."

—ELEANOR ROOSEVELT

While I may have a deep conceptual understanding of psychological safety, the scope of my experiential knowledge is limited. I have never overseen a large organization with a global footprint or faced leading *in extremis.* What are the boundaries of psychological safety, how is it affected by scale, and what does psychological safety look like in high-stakes arenas where people's lives hang in the balance? This chapter considers the construct through the lens of the US military.

In 1986, the movie *Top Gun* hit the big screen with a backdrop of the Cold War. The movie's main character, Maverick, a cocky, rebellious pilot, is sent to the Navy's Fighter Weapons School. The school aimed to revive the art of aerial dogfighting and develop graduates into superior fighter pilots.[1] I have a cousin who saw *Top Gun* and instantly knew what he would be when he grew up—a jet fighter pilot.

Colonel J.P. Boster went to the US Air Force Academy in 1987. We have had many discussions about leadership. Years ago, Boster told me his three leadership tenets are to be "approachable, credible, and humble." These servant-leader behaviors did not align with my assumptions about the military. Movies like *Full Metal Jacket*, *Apocalypse Now*, and characters like Colonel Jessup in *A Few Good Men* distorted my image of leadership in the armed services.

I interviewed Boster for this chapter. He has seen the full spectrum of leadership within the Air Force, beginning as an academy cadet, through numerous deployments, and as the fourteenth operations group commander at Columbus Air Force Base in Mississippi. In a wide-ranging conversation about leadership, the military, and being a pilot, we discussed:

- How does psychological safety play out in a large hierarchical organization?
- What is the role of "bootcamp" in fostering high-performing teams?
- How does the military culture of service to others reinforce stability and build cohesion?
- How does psychological safety affect communication in the cockpit?

NEVER LEAVE YOUR WINGMAN

Boster went to the academy when he was seventeen. I would have been thirteen. When we would gather for the holidays while he was away, I remember my aunt telling stories about all he was enduring. I vividly recall her talking about him eating with someone counting how many times he chewed. He was only allowed seven chews before he had to swallow.

You do not get training like this in private industry. Eating is a thoughtless act for most of us. How much discipline does it take to chew each bite only seven times? How much discipline does it take to lead when people's lives are on the line? At your next meal, I challenge you to try this exercise and see if you can shift your brain from autopilot while eating.

In 2011, the US Air Force Academy's commandant of cadets, Lieutenant General Richard M. Clark, wrote the foreword to *Developing Leaders of Character for the Twenty-First Century*, a foundational document for leadership training at the academy. In it, he explained that the academy's purpose is "to develop leaders of character who our nation can count on: leaders equipped to respond to the complexity, uncertainty, and asymmetry of today's world because they possess a firm and stable character that reflects the virtues embodied in our Core Values."[2]

In 2021, Superintendent Clark updated the Leaders of Character (LoC) framework. He describes the LoC as a "road map" for development, which the academy defines as "One's moral compass; the sum of those qualities of moral excellence which move a person to do the right thing despite pressures to the contrary."[3] The three pillars of the LoC are to live honorably, lift others, and elevate performance.

Living honorably is about exemplifying the Air Force's core values: Integrity First, Service Before Self, and Excellence in All We Do. Lifting others is the expectation to help others become their best version. Elevating performance is about self-actualizing to affect the common good.[4] While Boster's time at the academy predates the LoC, his stories reflect its leadership development lessons.

Boster explained how the indoctrination process at the academy strips everyone down to equals. "You all show up in the same pool, and they don't give a shit where you're from, what color you are, anything! It's like, here's the standard man, and you gotta meet the bar."

He explained how the process helped eliminate preconceived notions about his peers. Boster, raised in a small rural community in southern Illinois, initially detested another cadet from New Jersey. He did not like how he talked, dressed, or his mannerisms. In the vacuum created at the academy, it was "just a matter of figuring each other out, and when we got down to the bottom line, we realized we're about the same." Thirty years after graduating from the academy, Boster and his classmate from the Garden State remain friends and talk regularly.

Boster spoke about the pressure, isolation, and extreme challenges cadets face. Then he said something that, in hindsight, was so obvious. "The intent is not just to make sure we are all equals; you gotta turn to each other to try and survive. Who else can you talk to? You talked to the guy on your level—going through the same thing," he said. "That's where the teamwork starts." The shared dependency was how the students began to coalesce. Because the stakes are so much higher, it shouldn't or can't be easy. It was the foundation for building high-performing teams, but much more rigorous and challenging than most of us will ever experience.

In a sidebar titled "'Brutal Honesty' Is Still Brutal" in the book *Everybody Matters*, Chapman recalls speaking about leadership at The US Air Force Weapons School and participating in an after-action review of a flight training mission. Pilots refer to these debriefs as brutal honesty. "People go into a debriefing room to tell the pilot everything he could have done better," Chapman said. "They hold nothing back and criticize every single thing the pilot may have done less than perfectly."[5]

When I asked Boster about these reviews, he gave me a hypothetical scenario: You are a pilot who fails to utilize your plane's radar accurately. As a result, a bad guy snuck around, and your buddy gets shot down. "I mean, they don't rub your face in it too bad," Boster said, "but at the end of the day, they're going to write up on the board, 'Why did John die?' The answer is going to be Ted's radar work. Ted missed it."

Chapman is right about most workplaces. He suggests, "It is oppressive in any environment if all you talk about is the negative."[6] A fighter pilot's environment is distinctive. In most places, you are unlikely to pay for a mistake with your life. In most jobs, an error like overlooking a detail on a monitor doesn't mean someone is notifying your coworker's wife that they have been killed.

"That's what I really liked about being a fighter pilot," Boster said about the culture of accountability. "You can have your best friend look you in the eye and say, 'You fucked that up, and that's why we got our ass kicked.' That tuned us up to be on our A-game. Think of the culture, though. You're going to try your hardest every time you go out."

Remember the hypothetical scenario I described in chapter 3, where you overhear a manager criticizing someone for using filler words during a presentation? You might perceive the feedback to be critical or even degrading. In context, the supervisor or the employee may consider the feedback constructive or developmental. From Boster's point of view, the brutal honesty criticism is accurate, fair, and objective.

"That's the ultimate accountability," Boster explained. "It also becomes very trustworthy. I mean, it's not hostile. It is very fact-based, and if that's the standard, and you don't want to be that guy, it makes you better. I don't want to go back into that debrief and hear I got someone killed on a training mission. My radar work is going to be perfect."

The competition between the students for the top spot or Distinguished Graduate (DG) status in military schools impacts their career opportunities and potential promotions, which could make feedback contentious. Still, suppose you peel back the layers of perceived hostility and denigration. In that case, these after-action reviews exemplify the three pillars of the academy's LoC: to live honorably, lift others, and elevate performance. Despite the competitive setting, brutal honesty sessions are a learning environment where the pilots feel safe enough to be vulnerable and show their character to be receptive to criticism.

A unique brand of psychological safety is on display in these sessions. Boster explained it is about more than learning. It is about discipline, sacrifice, and self-preservation. "I mean being a fighter pilot is a kill or be-killed environment," Boster said. "When you get in a different environment, where no one is going to die, the rules can change."

SCALING CHARACTER AND CULTURE

I was curious about how psychological safety unfolded more generally within the Air Force. I perceived a rigid hierarchical structure. Pilots feel free to speak truth to each other, but are service men and women speaking truth to power up and down the chain of command? As we have established, having a sense of psychological safety has been shown to foster traits like empowerment, creativity, experimentation, and collaboration.

I asked Boster how psychological safety played out in the day-to-day life at the Air Force. He shared the military has numerous ways to glean great ideas from officers, enlisted ranks, and civilians. "I would tell you there's a little more room on the officer side to say, 'Really, why did we do it this way?'" He said there is less leeway for going off script on the typically young and inexperienced enlisted side, which represents about 90 percent of the Air Force.

I asked if there was a risk of stifling innovation and being stuck in the status quo. Boster clarified that enlisted men and women are encouraged to be innovative and provide ideas. Still, the enormity of running the daily operation can necessitate following the process. "If you're making wooden legs for hobby horses every day, it's likely been working for thirty years with the same template. I'm not saying somebody might not find a more efficient way to do it, but because of the scope of the operation, you can't have *E3 Johnny* coming to you every day saying, 'Hey boss, we need to do this a different way.'"

The chain of command can provide a clear hierarchy and structure that helps establish order and discipline. The security and predictability contribute to psychological safety, and individuals trust the value of service to others. The culture allows airmen to have confidence their superiors are in control and will make decisions that are in the group's best interests.

As Boster outlined the culture, it became clear the Air Force's core values are not espoused values; out of necessity, airmen live these values every day. "I was a maintenance officer for a while, too," Boster said. "It's just a different mentality in the Air Force. Even the young, enlisted guys are like, 'I'm going to fix this airplane so the bros that come on swing shift don't have to fix it.'" Boster pointed to the "bootcamp" process as the source of the mindset to serve others. "So, think back to the indoctrination: 'You guys are all trash.' You gotta love each other to survive because that's the only shoulder you have to cry on.'"

Psychological safety is the belief that you will not be punished or humiliated for speaking up with ideas, asking questions, expressing concerns, or making mistakes. It is the feeling that you can take risks and be vulnerable. The Air Force's values-driven culture mitigates much of the need for self-protection that normally inhibits psychological safety. It seems that people's fear of risk is more internal than external.

The pressure to not fail comes from the inside. "You don't ever want to be the person who comes up short because that means you're letting down one of your brothers. I mean, almost the worst insult you can get is, 'You didn't do your job, and you screwed this guy over,'" Boster explained. "To me, that's horrific."

At Boster's last stop before retiring, he had seven hundred pilots flying under him and fifteen hundred other people making the operation happen. "I'm the guy who says whether you graduate or not...For those pilots, it's career, life, or death." He felt a tremendous responsibility to ensure the people he passed were ready. Despite his top-dog job coming with prestige, perks, and power, "It's never about you," Boster said. "It's really about everybody else when you're on the top of the heap. Your life should be miserable. That's why you're there to make everyone else succeed or not, but it ain't about you."

PREVENTABLE FAILURE

For most of his career, Boster flew a single-seat F-15 fighter jet—one of military aviation's fastest, most maneuverable planes. After retiring from the Air Force, Boster joined FedEx and now flies Boeing 777 cargo planes across the Atlantic Ocean. The 777 is a stiff, sluggish, largely automated behemoth with twenty tons of freight in its belly. He said the difference was like "going from a bass boat to a cruise ship." It was a significant shift, not just in aircraft, now Boster was part of a team piloting the plane.

There is a link between psychological safety and pilot error. When team members do not feel psychologically safe, they may be less likely to speak about a potential hazard, even if they notice something that could lead to a mistake or accident. Cultures that repress employee voice can increase the risk of pilot error.

The National Transportation Safety Board found that 73 percent of the incidents in its database occurred on a crew's first day of flying together. They happened before people could experience how best to operate as a team—44 percent of those took place on a crew's first flight. Also, a NASA study found that fatigued crews with a history of working together made about half as many errors as those of rested pilots who had not previously flown together.[7]

These statistics did not surprise Boster. Every airline has protocols, "but when you fly with somebody for the first time, because the captain is the *big wheel,* things are subject to change," Boster said. "It should be standard where everybody can show up, get the flight plan, and do their thing. Because of people, it doesn't really work that way, so you don't know exactly what to expect from the other person until you have flown with them a couple of times."

In 1977, two Boeing 747 passenger jets collided on a runway on the Spanish island of Tenerife, resulting in 583 deaths. Crew Resource Management (CRM) training evolved from a 1979 workshop sponsored by NASA after the Tenerife disaster. Attendees identified that poor interpersonal communications, decision-making, and leadership contributed to air transport accidents.[8] CRM training aims to foster a culture of psychological safety and avoid preventable errors among aviation crews.

Boster explained CRM serves several purposes, and the biggest is "just because you're the highest-ranking guy in the cockpit doesn't mean you shouldn't take feedback from everyone else." He explained CRM is also about leveraging all available resources to make informed decisions when you need more information.

He used a crisis analogy to illustrate the point. "We just lost an engine over the Atlantic Ocean. Ted, what do you want to do? Do you want to go to Iceland, or do you want to try and make it to England?" It is about exploring all options. Your navigator may know something about a storm you don't, or if you call back to FedEx headquarters in Memphis, they could have critical insights. Captains cannot afford moments of narcissistic decision-making.

Boster described what my dad called giving everyone a voice but not a vote. You solicit information from everyone, but the "flip side of that is there's one guy with a hammer... eventually, there's going to be a decision made, and that's going to be the final decision." That hammer wielder is the captain. He is the only one with a vote, "but the idea is to get everyone's input and maybe make a smarter decision or prevent a stupid one."

LEADERS EAT LAST

I asked Boster if he missed being in the Air Force. After a long pause, he said, "I struggle with it, to be honest with you. I wanted to be a fighter pilot since I was a sophomore in high school. I got to do it, and I had the best time doing it....You just don't get to fly those kinds of machines and do that kind of flying, and for those who do, it is a brotherhood." He sounded like a retired professional athlete who didn't miss all the practice, preparation, politics, and strain on his family. However, he still needed the comradery and really missed game days.

After completing my interview with Boster, I circled back to Matt Whiat, the cofounder of the Chapman & Co. Leadership Institute, whom I interviewed for chapter 8. Whiat, a former US Air Force officer who once served as a bootcamp squadron commander, teaches leaders about Barry-Wehmiller's unique people-centered culture. He has a different perspective on the military's leadership development.

Today's military recruits are volunteers, and much of what happens in bootcamp is a holdover from the days of a conscript military when it was "critical to establish who was in charge," Whiat explained. "The idea of the training and breaking people down I find to be an antiquated mindset that actually harms the military... The training nowadays, I think, needs to be less focused on who is in charge and more on building character."

Whiat suggested that the military and civilian worlds are distinctive, but they could learn much from one another. For example, the military can dedicate time and resources to training and development because much of the costs are built in, whereas, in the private sector, it may be too resource dependent.

"No one in the military had to worry at night about making payroll, their people being poached by a competitor, or where they were going to find their next client," Whiat said. "The stressors and penalties for getting it wrong are different in both worlds, but the act of leadership—working with people toward a common objective in a way that preserves the dignity of people—is the same."

I contacted Tom Kolditz for his perspective on the role of "bootcamp" in developing teamwork and leadership. Kolditz is a retired brigadier general educator, author, prominent speaker, and leadership consultant specializing in crisis leadership and leading in extreme contexts. He agreed that pushing people out of their comfort zone is beneficial, but he described breaking people down as "superstitious." He said, "There is really no justification in breaking people down or stretching them to the point of failure. We know people learn better when they're not under that overall level of stress." Whiat and Kolditz pointed out a lack of leader development outcome measures for why the indoctrination process has remained the same.

Kolditz agreed with Boster's assertion that bootcamp can play a crucial role in helping build unity and a commitment to others that permeates the culture. "When individuals are under a common threat or common pressure, that does help develop teamwork and team attitudes."

Simon Sinek's book *Leaders Eat Last* is an homage to the military practice where the highest-ranking officers filled their plates last to ensure their troops were fed and cared for. In a YouTube video titled "The True Story Behind *Leaders Eat Last*," Sinek describes a dramatic experience he had while on a ride-along with the US Air Force during the war in Afghanistan. It helped him understand what it means to truly serve others.[9]

"You realize the power of community, the power of friendship, the power of a strong culture that is built on love, and I don't use that term lightly," Sinek said. "I've talked to the hardest of hardcore warriors, and I say, 'What is it that makes you good at what you do?' And they say, 'Love.' They love each other. We call each other colleagues and coworkers. They call each other brother and sister, and that relationship is real."[10]

While service men and women are busy defending our freedom, the private sector should consider what it would be like to work in an organization where you have absolute confidence that the rest of the team is willing to sacrifice themselves for the mission. Sinek highlights the contrast in approach and why our business strategy so often fails. "You know, in the military, they give medals to people who are willing to sacrifice themselves so that others may gain. In business, we give bonuses to people who are willing to sacrifice others so that we may gain. We have it backwards."[11]

KEY CHAPTER TAKEAWAYS

- Military leaders prioritize obligations to followers over their own needs.
- Maintaining psychological safety is always tenuous, but the context of the environment plays a role in what behaviors and communication trigger negative responses.
- The culture allows service men and women to trust that their superiors are in control and will make decisions in their best interests, making risk-taking and vulnerable behaviors safe.
- Relationships are the connective tissue that bonds the military. Members consider their peers family and are willing to sacrifice themselves for each other and the greater good of the mission.

CHAPTER 13:

BIG BROTHER
IS WATCHING

"Leadership is hard because, more than anything else, it's about people. Most of us struggle to manage ourselves: our subconscious drivers, our relationships, our emotions, our mental health, our habits. Leadership demands not only that we master ourselves, but also that we become strong enough and capable enough to help others do the same."

—MARTIN MOORE

Contextual factors have always complicated leading, but today we are experiencing a technological explosion. The resulting age of disruptive innovation will rival advances like the wheel, the printing press, the light bulb, and the cell phone.

What will the impact of today's technological revolution be on leadership? While a dystopian *Matrix*-like future may be improbable, we are already seeing concerns from creators and a recognition that adopting the technology is inevitable. "I view this possibility with a certain dreadful fascination," horror writer Stephen King said. "Would I forbid the teaching (if that is the word) of my stories to computers? Not even if I could."[1]

Acceptance, however, does not assuage fears. "If you want a picture of the future, imagine a boot stamping on a human face—forever."[2] George Orwell's *1984* quote represents today's concern about the unknown and a worst-case scenario of sentient Artificial Intelligence evolving without boundaries.

Theoretically, we are introducing a new invasive species into our ecosystem. AI's financial upside and competitive pressure will be too much to keep companies on the sidelines. A Big Data gold is inevitable. As leaders have more and more information at their disposal, will it tempt them to micromanage their charges? Will we see a revival of the 1950s and '60s command-and-control leadership style, or can we develop systems where the workers' experience and profits are not mutually exclusive? We are rapidly adopting this new power, and like any innovation or change intended to drive progress, we should be conscious of the potential for hidden downstream consequences.

The most cited definition of leadership is "a process whereby an individual influences a group of individuals to achieve a common goal."[3] What happens in an environment where there is no individual to do the influencing and decisions are driven solely by data and bots? Algorithms do not tolerate dissimilar learning curves, family crises, or illness. They do not accommodate outliers, aberrations, or temporary adversity.

While algorithms have the potential to maximize efficiency, they are built based on data fed in by people. Consequently, despite representing a façade of infallibility, those parameters can replicate human biases. Additionally, making decisions about employees solely on data can lead to commoditizing human beings and not accessing their full potential.

When working at 3PL, I took a chance on a candidate who was twice the age of our typical laborer. His résumé was mediocre, and he failed a math screening test. Yet, there was something about Joe. He was genuine, affable, and "just needed a chance." Initially, he struggled—mightily. His high order fill error rate affected our inventory accuracy and created additional work for the quality control and supervisory teams.

Joe's work was grueling, the technology was not user-friendly, and the environment was frequently inhospitable. Employees regularly worked forced overtime—multiple days of twelve-hour shifts—in a warehouse that was not temperature-controlled. There was no relief inside the facility on a soupy summer St. Louis day when the heat index exceeded one hundred degrees. In the winter, the landlord set the thermostat high enough to keep the fire protection system from freezing, but our employees did not receive the same consideration.

We chewed through new hires. Our annual turnover rate exceeded 108 percent. Many walked off the job, didn't finish training, or were fired for attendance or performance issues before their orientation period ended. I had terminated scores of people just like Joe. But not Joe, despite quality control, human resources, and my supervisory team voicing their concerns. Joe's learning curve was steep and long. When I left the company, he was one of our longest-tenured people. He never loaded the most trucks or picked the most cases, but he was likely the most dependable and accurate. What happens to people who "just needed a chance" in an AI-driven, data-only environment?

EARTH'S MOST CUSTOMER-CENTRIC COMPANY

Amazon has led the charge to make a buck by leveraging Big Data. One of my former logistics bosses retired from Amazon after working in one of its distribution centers. He explained, "In every aspect of the fulfillment process, actions and metrics are designed around customer satisfaction." He was responsible for a crushing amount of data and metrics intended to ensure a favorable customer experience. Information overload often led to more time managing his data than leading his people.

There is no second-guessing Amazon's business success and appeal to its customer base, but at times, Amazon's reliance on data and innovation has produced dubious results. In 2014, the growing company developed a talent search algorithm to automatically rank many candidates for job fit. Leaders created archetype candidate models for specific jobs based on standard terms appearing in past applications. Amazon fed its HR bot ten years' worth of résumé data, but programmers failed to account for the gender disparity in the male-dominated workforce. As a result, the algorithm taught itself that male candidates were desirable and discriminated against women.[4]

Amazon scrapped the program in 2018. However, the company has been attempting to resurrect its AI agent, Automated Applicant Evaluation. An internal document leaked in 2021 stated, "[T]he model is achieving precision comparable to that of the manual process and is not evidencing adverse impact." At the end of 2022, the company sent buyout offers to all low- and mid-level recruiters in its HR division.[5]

In November 2016, Amazon introduced Rekognition, an image recognition platform that touted accurate real-time facial analysis and identification by instantaneously comparing a user's image to a database containing millions of faces. The program held promise for multiple purposes, including identity verification and public safety applications.

To test the system's facial recognition accuracy, the ACLU of northern California scanned all 535 members of Congress. The software incorrectly identified twenty-eight members as having been arrested for a crime. Rekognition was found to perform poorly at identifying gender and had high error rates with black and brown people. A 2018 letter written by the ACLU stated, "Amazon should not be in the business of providing surveillance systems like Rekognition to the government."[6]

Rekognition continues today, as do its discrimination and civil liberty concerns.

In June 2021, a Bloomberg article highlighted a growing trend at the company by describing how a sixty-three-year-old Army veteran received an automated email terminating his employment. The bot tracking him found he'd failed to meet performance metrics.[7] The story highlights the type of unforeseen problems algorithms cannot account for. Performance impediments like traffic bottlenecks, road construction, accessing gated communities, or getting stuck behind a combine on a narrow rural road are all beyond a delivery driver's control. Every job in every industry has concealed challenges that bots cannot gauge. Yet, at Amazon, algorithms, with minimal human oversight review performance and terminate workers, according to the article.

In July 2021, a memo leaked about a perverse incentive structure for annual turnover known as the "Unregretted Attrition Rate" (UAR). Managers at Amazon have a target rate for yearly turnover, like the system developed by GE's CEO Jack Welch in the 1980s. GE's policy was dubbed *rank-and-yank* because it dealt with underperforming employees and managers by making termination decisions based on how they rated against their peers.

Similarly, Amazon's UAR differentiates high-performing employees from low-performing ones and ensures a healthy amount of attrition, voluntarily or through termination. The problem is Amazon managers were hiring people so they could later fire them.[8] This approach allowed managers to hit their metric with a sacrificial lamb rather than a current team member they may have built a relationship with or have knowledge of an extenuating circumstance.

My former boss had never witnessed Amazon's UAR policy, and his experience did not align with Amazon's villainous reputation. He told me, "I just didn't see many of the issues popularized via some sources in the media." He participated in frequent training at Amazon to encourage managers to be more employee centric. "In my experience, Amazon was genuine in listening to the 'voice of the associate' and provided managers with training to improve skills relative to employee engagement," he told me in an email. "Amazon routinely gave associates and managers the ability to rate their management experience anonymously... Those evaluations of manager skills were reported in aggregate and used by leadership and human resources to provide feedback." Managers could leverage constructive feedback to improve their performance ranking.

I am not suggesting these programs that leverage data and technology are inherently wrong or run counter to healthy employees and work cultures. Nor am I hopping on the "Amazon is a villain" bandwagon. I would argue that Big Data can help deliver benefits beyond shareholder value if those advantages are prioritized and factored into the business calculus. When we delegate leadership decisions to machines, information gets processed as one plus one equals two. Leadership is more nuanced.

Because a work culture is greater than the sum of its parts and it moderates organizational performance, how employees make sense of their environment matters. As we've seen, a leader plays a crucial role in this interpretation and can help prevent misunderstandings between employees' perceptions and reality. A bot cannot.

WHAT CAN BROWN DO FOR YOU?

Even programs with substantial, measurable benefits to the greater good can negatively affect the workforce. In 2012, UPS launched its on-road integrated optimization and navigation (ORION) system to reduce delivery miles and fuel consumption. Its website touts, "Since ORION's initial deployment, it has saved UPS about one hundred million miles and ten million gallons of fuel per year."[9] Beyond the enormous economic benefit, UPS estimates that it has reduced one hundred thousand metric tons of CO_2 emissions.[10]

In the days before ORION and before Google Maps lived on a smartphone in everyone's pocket, I was a

UPS driver. I did not have enough seniority to have a dedicated route, so I spent much of each day lost. I leafed through a dog-eared spiral-bound map book for hours to get directions. In the old days, drivers mitigated this challenge and gained efficiency by acquiring area knowledge once they had a dedicated route. For example, if you know someone is your only stop outside of town, but they are a receptionist at the dentist's office, you can also deliver their packages when you are at the dentist.

To understand the scope of a driver's learning curve, consider that I made 120–130 delivery stops on any given day. The route combinations a driver could choose are virtually infinite. Today, technology mitigates that challenge. ORION processes over three hundred million data points and delivers tens of thousands of real-time route optimizations each minute. Drivers simply follow the instructions from their handheld devices.

UPS drivers no longer face a blank canvas; their days have become paint-by-numbers. I see tremendous value in optimization, turn-by-turn navigation, workload leveling, and reducing UPS's environmental footprint, but what does ORION's implementation mean for package drivers?

Researchers define perceived organizational support as employees' "general beliefs concerning how much the organization values their contributions and cares about their well-being."[11] These perceptions profoundly affect employees' outlook and behaviors and are critical to creating a climate that promotes psychological safety.

What does it do to an individual's psyche to have GPS constantly tracking your behavior? How did ORION's implementation affect the smallest component of the system—the individual employee? Do they feel psychologically safe?

I reached out to someone I worked with at UPS to learn about the transition to ORION. We started loading trucks together on the 3 a.m. shift, and eventually, we both were behind the wheel of big brown package delivery trucks until I left the company.

My former colleague explained that while the project was in development for years, the rollout to drivers happened abruptly. "It wasn't like they brought it in and said, 'Hey, we're going to test this.' It was, 'Hey, this is the new system. Figure it out.'" He remembered system bugs hampering the launch. "I guess, really looking at it, I don't know how you would test that system on that big of a scale anyhow, but there were issues. There still are issues with that system."

Despite the chaos ORION caused drivers, I assumed the process would be seamless for the customer. "The customer saw a shit-ton of disruption," he told me. Historically, drivers built relationships with and would make accommodations for customers like hospitals and auto shops waiting on medication or a critical part. Drivers used their judgment to be more efficient. Delivering to stops with a futon mattress, flat-screen TV, or Walmart's 115 packages allowed us to move freely within the truck. Not with ORION. "It wasn't about the customer anymore. It was only about the efficiency of how they were reducing miles and reducing gas," he told me. "It didn't matter that a company for thirty-five years had been the third stop on your route, and you were there by 8:53 every day. With ORION, you might not get there until three minutes before they close."

As a driver, I would deliver my priority Next Day Air packages and then begin my route. My friend said that expectation had changed. "Because this Next Day Air is taking you down a street that you have three other stops, which are loaded on the back top shelf that you can't even get to, you're supposed to climb and dig, and you're wasting time." Between these inefficiencies and dealing with disgruntled customers, he wondered how UPS could ever realize a return on its investment.

I asked him how being under a constant microscope affected the drivers' psychological safety. He explained that the impact was negligible because the environment was already toxic. It just created more opportunities for flashpoints. He said, "I'm sure some report got printed out from corporate, and they have to come and ask, 'Why did you back up here?' Well, that's because I have to go down this little lane that's the size for a Go-Kart. I have a giant UPS truck, and it's going to mean a twelve-point turnaround."

He acknowledged the system's intent—for example, more accidents happen while backing; however, managers frequently question drivers for subjective things. He explained, "ORION thinks you can go fifty-five miles an hour down this road. Well, it does not know it is a country road that is so rough if you go over thirty-five miles an hour, you're going to bounce the truck into the ditch."

So, how did ORION's implementation affect employees and their sense of psychological safety?

At least one driver has a dubious perception of the results. "There wasn't one care in the world about what this was going to do to the drivers, and not much thought was put into what it was going to mean to the customer. This was more of a question of how do we cut costs? How can we save? I get that's what you do to succeed in business, but at some point, you still have to value your employees and customers."

THE GREATER GOOD

In the illustrations above, the adoption of technology primarily benefited shareholders. Could AI facilitate a transition away from shareholder capitalism to stakeholder capitalism by reducing the investment needed to support employees? AI has proved to be effective at boosting employee well-being with its ability to efficiently sift through endless data, which would overwhelm a traditional HR department.

Predictive analytics powered by AI can help identify workplace wellness trends like employee burnout, ergonomic problems, health risks, and other well-being challenges employees face. AI chatbots can also become cost-effective frontline resources for employees to get answers or early interventions. Platforms like Affectiva, Headspace, and Woebot offer AI-driven mental health support.[12]

In a Kellogg School of Management blog, Hatim Rahman, an assistant professor of management and organizations, suggests that our fear of AI is largely unfounded. While some creative industries have lost work to generative AI, the transition to new technology is not as disruptive as it feels. Rahman points out that of the 270 jobs listed in the 1950 census, automation has only eliminated one—elevator operator.[13]

Rahman says that because of the resources required to adopt AI, "It's going to take a long time for it to penetrate an industry, especially in ways that will affect your career." And because we have this lead time, it allows us to choose how we adopt new technology. He gives the example of the airline industry. Today, as much as 90 percent of a pilot's responsibilities are automated, but we choose to have humans at the controls in case something goes wrong. "We can choose to use AI to replace as many workers as possible—or we can instead choose to use AI to bolster talent and identify it in underrecognized places," Rahman says. "We can choose to let machines make the bulk of the decisions around our healthcare, education, and defense—or we can choose to keep humans at the helm, ensuring that human values and priorities rule the day."[14]

While fear of the unknown generally makes people resist change, business and technology leaders remained bullish on the future of AI. Bill Gates compared the emergence of AI to the impact of agricultural advancements. People were also anxious about new technology in the early 1900s, but innovation led to new opportunities. "We're way better off than when everybody was doing farm work," he said. "This will be like that."[15]

Technology leaders are optimistic but acknowledge we still have work to do, and the stakes are high. Google's SVP of research, technology, and society, James Manyika, suggested, "People understand that AI will disrupt their lives—but they hope it's for the better. We must not let them down."[16]

Whether it is a government, business and social leaders, IT companies, or some sentient machine of the future, we must always consider the risk of giving the power of leadership to entities that can control people rather than serve them.

KEY CHAPTER TAKEAWAYS

- AI's financial upside and competitive pressure will be too much to keep companies on the sidelines.
- Leaders are necessary to interpret context and can help prevent misunderstandings between employees' perceptions and reality. A bot cannot.

- Technology can positively affect employee well-being by efficiently sifting through endless data to identify workplace wellness trends such as employee burnout, ergonomic problems, health risks, and other challenges.
- We have time to choose where AI's presence is an asset because adopting it is a slow, resource-dependent process.
- We must consider risks when we delegate the power of leadership to entities that can control people rather than serve them.

CONCLUSION

Leaders controlling people rather than serving them brings us full circle to my reason for going back to school. As a scholar, I wanted to better understand the toxic work environments I had experienced. More importantly, as a leader, I wanted to know how to change them.

At the opening weekend of my PhD program, hearing Dr. Edmondson discuss her research—the epiphany that the high-performing nurses were not making more mistakes; errors were just surfacing because the culture allowed them to be vulnerable, learn from failure, and collaborate—started a journey that transformed how I understood leadership.

During my evolution, psychological safety evolved rapidly, too. Not long ago, it was a revelation in an inconspicuous academic paper. However, as scholars identified more and more positive outcomes of psychological safety, research accelerated. Psychological safety has become a viral business buzzword that can be misused or taken out of context. Psychological safety is neither a panacea nor a comfortable consensus, maintaining harmony, or being nice.

Psychological safety's magic is its simplicity. It emerges from the signals leaders send and the way employees interpret those cues. Are employees making sense of their leaders' behavior and other environmental signals such as creating a safe place to challenge each other so the best solutions can surface?

Over my career, I have sat in many leadership meetings and discussed trust: What does trust feel like in this workplace? Why is it declining? Why does one team seem to have it but not another? We should have been discussing *whether we are doing things that allow employees to perceive us as trustworthy*. Leaders desire the reciprocal of trust—the engagement, empowerment, and innovation that surface when workers trust their leaders, develop relationships, and feel psychologically safe enough to risk vulnerability and take action.

The reasons for promoting psychological safety go beyond improved organizational outcomes. In October 2022, US Surgeon General Vivek Murthy, MD, published the office's first-ever Surgeon General's Framework for Workplace Mental Health and Well-Being. Dr. Murthy specifically stated that leaders should protect workers from harm by prioritizing psychological safety. "Creating the conditions for physical and psychological safety is a critical foundation for ensuring mental health and well-being in the workplace." The report highlighted that encouraging employee voice behavior is vital. "Creating an environment where workers' voices are supported without fear of job loss or retaliation is an essential component of healthy organizations."[1]

Fostering psychological safety is the best way to get the most out of our employees, but it is also in their best interest. Social scientists now suggest psychological safety is a basic human need that applies beyond the workplace and is a "prerequisite for people to be at their best in all aspects of life."[2]

GOOGLE IT

In 2012, Google's people analytics team determined the secrets of effective teams. The effort was code-named Project Aristotle, a tribute to Aristotle's quote, "The whole is greater than the sum of its parts." The initiative took over two years, included interviews with hundreds of Google employees, and analyzed data from over 180 active Google teams.[3]

The project's sponsors expected to uncover a recipe to assemble the best teams. "We were pretty confident that we'd find the perfect mix of individual traits and skills necessary for a stellar team—take one Rhodes Scholar, two extroverts, one engineer who rocks at AngularJS, and a PhD. Voila. Dream team assembled, right?" Julia Rozovsky, the lead researcher, explained. "We were dead wrong. Who is on a team matters less than how the team members interact, structure their work, and view their contributions."[4]

Ultimately, Project Aristotle identified five traits of Google's high-performing teams:

- "Psychological safety: Can we take risks on this team without feeling insecure or embarrassed?

- Dependability: Can we count on each other to do high quality work on time?
- Structure & clarity: Are goals, roles, and execution plans on our team clear?
- Meaning of work: Are we working on something personally important for each of us?
- Impact of work: Do we fundamentally believe that our work matters?"[5]

Rozovsky states, "Psychological safety was far and away the most important of the five dynamics we found—it's the underpinning of the other four."[6]

Will Google continue to value and integrate Project Aristotle's learnings about high-performing teams and the role of psychological safety? Will machine learning leave any room for team learning?

THE FUTURE OF PSYCHOLOGICAL SAFETY

In chapter 5, I discussed how the foundation of relational leadership theory is informal agreements between employees and employers. Each party makes sense of the relationship through a cost-benefit analysis. Many organizations and leaders have breached those social contracts. Employees make sense of our behaviors and find us wanting—leaving them wanting out.

A 2020 report found that attracting and retaining talent was CEO's number one issue. The report suggests that "wrong leadership [may be a] top reason for toxic work culture."[7] A study published in the *MIT Sloan*

Management Review found a toxic work culture is 10.4 times more potent than compensation in predicting employee turnover. "Toxic culture is the biggest factor pushing employees out the door."[8]

What is the solution? Even when employment satisfies people's basic needs like accessing food, shelter, and having a sense of security, they desire more. If employees do not perceive an organization supporting their quest to satisfy higher-order needs like inclusion, sensing accomplishment, and achieving one's potential, it drives discontent.

Matt Poepsel, a consultant specializing in talent optimization, describes this reality as the Killer Bs. He says people seek "Being, Belonging, and something Bigger than myself. I call these *Killer Bs* because when we fail to satisfy them, it kills our productivity, engagement, performance, and intent to stay."[9]

Psychological safety is an individual impression—an absence of fear and a willingness to be vulnerable and contribute when it is risk-free to do nothing. While it is a personal experience, the construct's most significant effects emerge in groups. Psychologically safe teams assume good intentions, deal with conflict productively, and prioritize the mission over self-protection. They strive for the best outcomes, not comfortable consensus.

THE EASY WAY OR THE HARD WAY?

In the first chapter, I introduced a relational model for leading, the competing values framework, and I shared some parenting challenges I have had with my daughter that frequently led to me saying, "We can do this the easy way or the hard way." Regrettably, I have also led that way for much of my career.

Douglas McGregor expressed this view of human nature in two assumptions he saw in leaders. Theory X represents a leader who micromanages or coerces employees because of a pessimistic opinion of people, assuming they are lazy or dishonest. In contrast, Theory Y leaders have an optimistic opinion of their people and assume employees have good intentions.[10]

Having led with both approaches, I have found that it takes more patience, commitment, and courage to be optimistic and trust people. However, the rewards of building relationships, helping people reach their potential, and achieving common goals are priceless.

Behavioral profiles suggest I am introverted and more focused on tasks than relationships. An interpersonal approach may come more naturally for extroverted leaders who thrive socially. This contrast illustrates why leadership is enigmatic.

Bruce Avolio, a management professor at the University of Washington and executive director of the Center for Leadership and Strategic Thinking, says, "Leadership is a function of both the leader and the led and the complexity of the context."[11] I believe the four-step relational model from chapter 1 can help leaders understand this puzzle Avolio alludes to.

When leading yourself, you understand your biases, motivations, and values, so you can be mindful of how people make sense of your behaviors. This awareness is crucial because when you are leading others, you are responsible for the shadow your behaviors cast over the entire organization. They are the primary input in employees' sensemaking process, and it is the only piece of the leadership puzzle you fully control. That is why I titled this book *Walk Your Talk*.

The fostering psychological safety model outlined in chapter 11 will help you with the third step, engineering culture. The model emphasizes a connection to purpose, alignment of values, and elevation of commitment. It creates opportunities for continuous improvement and allows you to adapt—regardless of the environment—because of its relational foundation.

As Google learned, there is no magic formula. The contributors on a team matter little. Performance comes from how the team interacts. Whether you are in a veterinary clinic, a warehouse, a manufacturing plant, an Air Force post-flight review, or a high-performing team at Google, feeling psychologically safe in one's environment promotes individual and organizational achievement.

This book is a recipe for executing strategy through leader behaviors that build psychologically safe work cultures.

Now, go walk your talk.

ACKNOWLEDGMENTS

Lindsay, Nolan, and Vail, thank you for your patience, sacrifices, and encouragement throughout this process. I could not have made it to the finish line without your love and support.

Amy Edmondson, thank you for serving on my dissertation committee. Your research and knowledge have made me a better leader and person.

The people who I interviewed brought drab academic content to life with their stories and insights. Thank you for sharing Ron Riggio, J.P. Boster, Tom Kolditz, Matt Whiat, "Wall Street," and my colleagues from UPS, 3PL, and Amazon who also chose to remain anonymous.

Beta readers were critical in making this book viable. Dozens of people waded through crappy early chapters to provide priceless feedback. A few brave souls—Katy Huebner, Carolyn Boster, Gary Dollar, Mike Montgomery, Colleen Lyons, and Amber Johnson—endured large sections of the rough draft or the entire manuscript.

Supporters of my presale campaign believed in this book when it was in its infancy. Thank you: Mike Bailey, Craig Bengtson, Jeff and Rachel Bilyeu, Kirk and Isle Boster, Sally Boutelle, Tony Catlett, Lela DeToye, Gary and Gale Dollar, Kevin Drollinger, Emily Gates, David and Kathy Hall, Amber Johnson, Scott and Kristen Manny, Gary Meyer, Lee Murphy, Amber Spaur, Francisco Vazquez Jr., and Kathie Winter.

ENDNOTES

INTRODUCTION

1. Deborah Ancona, "Sensemaking: Framing and Acting in the Unknown," in *The Handbook for Teaching Leadership: Knowing, Doing, and Being*, ed. Scott Snook, Nitin Nohria, and Rakesh Khurana (New York, NY: Sage Publications, 2011), 3.

2. Mikhail M. Bakhtin, "The Dialogic Imagination: Four Essays," trans. Caryl Emerson and Michael Holquist, *Slavic Review* 41, no. 3 (January 1982): 580–581, https://doi.org/10.2307/2497064.

3. Larry E. Senn and Jim Hart, *Winning Teams—Winning Cultures* (Santa Barbara, CA: Leaders Press, 2006).

4. Edgar H. Schein, *Organizational Culture and Leadership* (San Francisco CA: Jossey-Bass Publishers, 1985), 33–34.

5. B. V. Moore, "The May Conference on Leadership," *Personnel Journal* 6 (1927): 124–128.

6. Russ Marion and Mary Uhl Bien, "Leadership in Complex Organizations," *The Leadership Quarterly* 12, no. 4

(December 2001): 389–418, https://doi.org/10.1016/s1048-9843(01)00092-3.

7. Kelsey Lynett Ford, Michael Menchine, Elizabeth Burner, Sanjay Arora, Kenji Inaba, Demetrios Demetriades, and Bertrand Yersin, "Leadership and Teamwork in Trauma and Resuscitation," *The Western Journal of Emergency Medicine* 17, no. 5 (September 2016): 549–556, https://doi.org/10.5811/westjem.2016.7.29812.

8. Amy C. Edmondson, "Managing the Risk of Learning: Psychological Safety in Work Teams," in *International Handbook of Organizational Teamwork and Cooperative Working,* ed. Michael West, Dean Tjosvold, and Ken G. Smith (Hoboken, NJ: Wiley eBooks, 2003), https://doi.org/10.1002/9780470696712.ch13.

9. Walter Isaacson, *Elon Musk* (New York, NY: Simon and Schuster, 2023), 508.

10. Douglas McGregor, "The Human Side of Enterprise," in *Leadership and Motivation, Essays of Douglas McGregor,* ed. Warren G. Bennis and Edgar H. Schein (Cambridge, MA: MIT Press, 1966), 3–20.

11. Jim Harter, "In New Workplace, US Employee Engagement Stagnates," *Workplace* (blog), *Gallup,* June 6, 2024, https://www.gallup.com/workplace/608675/new-workplace-employee-engagement-stagnates.aspx.

12. Bob Chapman, "The Value of Identifying Values," *Barry-Wehmiller's Blog* (blog), April 17, 2013, https://www.

barrywehmiller.com/post/blog/2020/03/05/the-value-of-identifying-values.

Chapter 1

1. John Pitonyak and Rob DeSimone, "How to Engage Frontline Managers," *Workplace* (blog), *Gallup*, January 19, 2024, https://www.gallup.com/workplace/395210/engage-frontline-managers.aspx.

2. Edgar H. Schein, *Organizational Culture and Leadership* (San Francisco, CA: Jossey Bass Publishers, 1985), 33–34.

3. John Pitonyak and Rob DeSimone, "How to Engage Frontline Managers," *Workplace* (blog), *Gallup*, January 19, 2024, https://www.gallup.com/workplace/395210/engage-frontline-managers.aspx.

Chapter 2

1. Alannah E. Rafferty and Simon Lloyd D. Restubog, "The Influence of Abusive Supervisors on Followers' Organizational Citizenship Behaviours: The Hidden Costs of Abusive Supervision," *British Journal of Management* 22, no. 2 (December 2010): 270–285, https://doi.org/10.1111/j.1467-8551.2010.00732.x.

2. Mary Mawritz, David M. Mayer, Jenny M. Hoobler, Sandy J. Wayne, and Sophia V. Marinova, "A Trickle Down Model of Abusive Supervision," *Personnel Psychology* 65, no. 2 (May 2012): 325–357, https://doi.org/10.1111/j.1744-6570.2012.01246.x.

3. Amy C. Edmondson and Zhike Lei, "Psychological Safety: The History, Renaissance, and Future of an Interpersonal Construct," *Annual Review of Organizational Psychology and Organizational Behavior* 1, no. 1 (March 2014): 23–43, https://doi.org/10.1146/annurev-orgpsych-031413-091305.

Chapter 3

1. South African History Online, "M.K. Gandhi Is Forcibly Removed from a Whites-Only Train Carriage," *South African History Online's Blog* (blog), June 6, 2021, https://www.sahistory.org.za/dated-event/mk-gandhi-forcibly-removed-whites-only-train-carriage.

2. Martin Luther King Jr., *Stride toward Freedom: The Montgomery Story* (San Francisco, CA: Harper, 1958), 79.

3. Shannon C., "5 Things to Know: Surprising Facts about Martin Luther King Jr.," *Stories* (blog), National Museum of African American History and Culture, September 20, 2021, https://nmaahc.si.edu/explore/stories/5-things-know-surprising-facts.

4. Adam Toren, "3 Important Leadership Lessons from Dr. Martin Luther King, Jr," *Leadership* (blog), *Entrepreneur*, January 16, 2023, https://www.entrepreneur.com/leadership/3-important-leadership-lessons-from-dr-martin-luther-king/230958.

5. Psychology Today Staff, "First Impressions," *Basics* (blog), *Psychology Today*, July 11, 2024, https://www.psychologytoday.com/us/basics/first-impressions.

6. Edward L. Thorndike, "A Constant Error in Psychological Ratings," *Journal of Applied Psychology* 4, no. 1 (March 1920): 25–29, https://doi.org/10.1037/h0071663.

7. Nalini Ambady and Robert Rosenthal, "Thin Slices of Expressive Behavior as Predictors of Interpersonal Consequences: A Meta-analysis," *Psychological Bulletin* 111, no. 2 (March 1992): 256–274, https://doi.org/10.1037/0033-2909.111.2.256.

8. Albert Mehrabian and Morton Wiener, "Decoding of Inconsistent Communications," *Journal of Personality and Social Psychology* 6, no. 1 (January 1967): 109–114, https://doi.org/10.1037/h0024532.

9. Carol Kinsey Goman, "The Incredible Power of Paralinguistic Communication: How You Say What You Say Matter," *Companies* (blog), *BBN Times*, April 8, 2023, https://www.bbntimes.com/companies/the-incredible-power-of-paralinguistic-communication-how-you-say-what-you-say-matter.

10. Marianna Pogosyan, "Non-Verbal Communication across Cultures: When Our Gestures Speak Louder than Our Words," *Body Language* (blog), *Psychology Today*, November 7, 2019, https://www.psychologytoday.com/us/blog/between-cultures/201706/non-verbal-communication-across-cultures.

11. Sarah Mohamed, "The Rules for Eating with Your Hands in India, Africa, and the Middle East," *World Cuisines* (blog), *Food Republic*, April 15, 2024, https://www.foodrepublic.com/1294459/rules-for-eating-with-your-hands/.

12. Doha News Team, "#Qtip: Why Arabs Don't Like to Use Their Left Hands," *Doha News*, April 20, 2017, https://dohanews.co/qtip-why-arabs-dont-like-to-use-their-left-hands-2/.

13. Michael Argyle and Mark Cook, *Gaze and Mutual Gaze* (Cambridge, UK: Cambridge University Press, 1976).

14. Helmut Morsbach, "Aspects of Nonverbal Communication in Japan," *The Journal of Nervous and Mental Disease* 157, no. 4 (October 1973): 262–77, https://doi.org/10.1097/00005053-197310000-00006.

15. James R. Detert and Ethan R. Burris, "Leadership Behavior and Employee Voice: Is the Door Really Open?" *The Academy of Management Journal* 50, no. 4 (August 2007): 869–884, https://doi.org/10.5465/amj.2007.26279183.

16. Jennifer J. Kish-Gephart, James R. Detert, Linda Klebe Treviño, and Amy C. Edmondson, "Silenced by Fear: The Nature, Sources, and Consequences of Fear at Work," *Research in Organizational Behavior* 29 (January 2009): 163–193, https://doi.org/10.1016/j.riob.2009.07.002.

17. Amy C. Edmondson, "Psychological Safety and Learning Behavior in Work Teams," *Administrative Science Quarterly* 44, no. 2 (June 1999): 350–383, https://doi.org/10.2307/2666999.

18. Frances J. Milliken, Elizabeth Wolfe Morrison, and Patricia Faison Hewlin, "An Exploratory Study of Employee Silence: Issues That Employees Don't Communicate Upward and Why," *Journal of Management Studies* 40, no. 6 (August 2003): 1453–1476, https://doi.org/10.1111/1467-6486.00387.

19. Amy C. Edmondson, "Psychological Safety, Trust, and Learning in Organizations: A Group-Level Lens," in *Trust and Distrust in Organizations: Dilemmas and Approaches*, ed. Roderick Kramer and Karen Cook (New York, NY: Russell Sage Foundation, 2004), 239–282.

20. Ingrid M. Nembhard and Amy C. Edmondson, "Making It Safe: The Effects of Leader Inclusiveness and Professional Status on Psychological Safety and Improvement Efforts in Health Care Teams," *Journal of Organizational Behavior* 27, no. 7 (September 2006): 941–966, https://doi.org/10.1002/job.413.

21. Amy C. Edmondson, "Learning from Mistakes Is Easier Said Than Done: Group and Organizational Influences on the Detection and Correction of Human Error," *Journal of Applied Behavioral Science* 40, no. 1 (March 2004): 66–90, https://doi.org/10.1177/0021886304263849.

22. Bethany C. Bray, Roseanne J. Foti, Nicole J. Thompson, and Sarah F. Wills, "Disentangling the Effects of Self Leader Perceptions and Ideal Leader Prototypes on Leader Judgments Using Loglinear Modeling with Latent Variables," *Human Performance* 27, no. 5 (October 2014): 393–415, https://doi.org/10.1080/08959285.2014.956176.

23. Frances J. Milliken, Elizabeth Wolfe Morrison, and Patricia Faison Hewlin, "An Exploratory Study of Employee Silence: Issues That Employees Don't Communicate Upward and Why," *Journal of Management Studies* 40, no. 6 (August 2003): 1453–1476, https://doi.org/10.1111/1467-6486.00387.

24. Jennifer J. Kish-Gephart, James R. Detert, Linda Klebe Treviño, and Amy C. Edmondson, "Silenced by Fear: The Nature, Sources, and Consequences of Fear at Work," *Research in Organizational Behavior* 29 (January 2009): 163–193, https://doi.org/10.1016/j.riob.2009.07.002.

25. Luke Norris, "How Charles Barkley's Controversial 'I Am Not a Role Model' Nike Spot Came to Be," *NBA* (blog), *SportsCasting*, April 13, 2020, https://www.sportscasting.com/how-charles-barkleys-controversial-i-am-not-a-role-model-nike-spot-came-to-be/.

26. Will Starjacki, "'We Got Too Many Black Kids That Think They Can Only Be Successful through Athletics'— Charles Barkley Shares Why He Did the Infamous 'I Am Not a Role Model' Commercial with Nike," *Old School* (blog), *Basketball Network*, April 5, 2023, https://www.basketballnetwork.net/old-school/charles-barkley-shares-why-he-did-the-infamous-i-am-not-a-role-modelcommercial-with-nike.

27. Ibid.

Chapter 4

1. J. Kiley Hamlin, "Moral Judgment and Action in Preverbal Infants and Toddlers: Evidence for an Innate Moral Core," *Current Directions in Psychological Science* 22, no. 3 (June 2013): 186–193, https://doi.org/10.1177/0963721412470687.

2. J. William Pfeiffer, *Theories and Models in Applied Behavioral Science: Group* (Zurich, CH: Pfeiffer & Co, 1991).

3. Ibid.

4. Patrick M. Lencioni, *The Five Dysfunctions of a Team: A Leadership Fable, 20th Anniversary Edition* (Hoboken, NJ: John Wiley & Sons, 2010), 195.

5. Hogan Assessments, "What Is Personality? Identity Versus Reputation," *Hogan Assessments* (blog), March 25, 2022, https://www.hoganassessments.com/blog/what-is-personality-identity-reputation/.

6. Kenwyn K. Smith and David N. Berg, *Paradoxes of Group Life: Understanding Conflict, Paralysis, and Movement in Group Dynamics* (Hoboken, NJ: Jossey-Bass, 1997).

7. Ibid.

8. Brené Brown, "Dare to Lead | Authenticity Is a Collection of Choices That We Have to Make Every Day," *Brené Brown's Blog* (blog), November 14, 2023, https://brenebrown.com/art/authenticity-is-a-collection-of-choices/.

Chapter 5

1. James R. Detert and Linda K. Treviño, "Speaking up to Higher-Ups: How Supervisors and Skip-Level Leaders Influence Employee Voice," *Organization Science* 21, no. 1 (February 2010): 249–270, https://doi.org/10.1287/orsc.1080.0405.

2. David L. Scruton, *Sociophobics: The Anthropology of Fear* (Boulder, CO: Westview Press, 1986), 7.

3. Arne Öhman and Susan Mineka, "Fears, Phobias, and Preparedness: Toward an Evolved Module of Fear and Fear Learning," *Psychological Review* 108, no. 3 (January 2001): 483–522, https://doi.org/10.1037/0033-295x.108.3.483.

4. Jennifer J. Kish-Gephart, James R. Detert, Linda Klebe Treviño, and Amy C. Edmondson, "Silenced by Fear: The Nature, Sources, and Consequences of Fear at Work," *Research in Organizational Behavior* 29 (January 2009): 163–93, https://doi.org/10.1016/j.riob.2009.07.002.

5. Ibid.

6. Judith Meinert and Nicole C. Krämer, "How the Expertise Heuristic Accelerates Decision-Making and Credibility Judgments in Social Media by Means of Effort Reduction," *PLOS ONE* 17, no. 3 (March 2022): e0264428, https://doi.org/10.1371/journal.pone.0264428.

7. Indiana University School of Medicine, "Definitions | Honor Code | IU School of Medicine," About, Indiana University School of Medicine, accessed August 8, 2024, https://medicine.iu.edu/about/policies-guidelines/honor-code/definitions.

8. Amos Tversky and Daniel Kahneman, "Judgment under Uncertainty: Heuristics and Biases," *Science* 185, no. 4157 (September 1974): 1124–31, https://doi.org/10.1126/science.185.4157.1124.

9. Hershey H. Friedman, "Cognitive Biases and Their Influence on Critical Thinking and Scientific Reasoning: A Practical Guide for Student and Teachers," *Social Science*

Research Network (January 2017): https://doi.org/10.2139/ssrn.2958800.

10. Kassiani Nikolopoulou, "The Availability Heuristic | Example & Definition," *Research Bias* (blog), *Scribbr*, March 6, 2023, https://www.scribbr.com/research-bias/availability-heuristic/.

11. PETA Staff, "Lawn Mowers, Tanning Beds, and Twenty-Plus Other Things That Kill More People than Shark Encounters," *Features* (blog), PETA, July 27, 2023, https://www.peta.org/features/shark-attack-vs-other-causes-of-death/.

12. Timur Kuran and Cass R. Sunstein, "Availability Cascades and Risk Regulation," *Stanford Law Review* 51, no. 4 (April 1999): 683, https://doi.org/10.2307/1229439.

13. John Stossel, *Give Me a Break: How I Exposed Hucksters, Cheats, and Scam Artists and Became the Scourge of the Liberal Media...* (New York, NY: HarperCollins Publishers), 75.

14. Jeffrey Sanford Russell, John Hawthorne, and Lara Buchak, "Groupthink," *Philosophical Studies* 172, no. 5 (July 2014): 1287–1309, https://doi.org/10.1007/s11098-014-0350-8.

15. Kim S. Cameron, Carlos Mora, Trevor Leutscher, and Margaret Calarco, "Effects of Positive Practices on Organizational Effectiveness," *Journal of Applied Behavioral Science* 47, no. 3 (January 2011): 266–308, https://doi.org/10.1177/0021886310395514.

16. Jason T. Newsom, Masami Nishishiba, David L. Morgan, and Karen S. Rook, "The Relative Importance of Three

Domains of Positive and Negative Social Exchanges: A Longitudinal Model with Comparable Measures," *Psychology and Aging* 18, no. 4 (December 2003): 746–754, https://doi.org/10.1037/0882-7974.18.4.746.

17. Stephen R. Flora, "Praise's Magic Reinforcement Ratio: Five to One Gets the Job Done," *The Behavior Analyst Today* 1, no. 4 (January 2000): 64–69, https://doi.org/10.1037/h0099898.

18. Robert Folger and Russell Cropanzano, "Fairness Theory: Justice as Accountability," in *Advances in Organizational Justice*, ed. Jerald Greenberg (Stanford, CA: Stanford University Press, 2002), 1–55.

19. Quinetta M. Roberson, "Justice in Teams: The Activation and Role of Sensemaking in the Emergence of Justice Climates," *Organizational Behavior and Human Decision Processes* 100, no. 2 (July 2006): 177–192, https://doi.org/10.1016/j.obhdp.2006.02.006.

20. Daniel Goleman, "Leadership That Gets Results," in *Leadership Perspectives*, ed. by Alan Hooper (Oxfordshire, UK: *Routledge eBooks*, 2017), 85–96, https://doi.org/10.4324/9781315250601-9.

21. Amy C. Edmondson and Edgar H. Schein, *Teaming: How Organizations Learn, Innovate, and Compete in the Knowledge Economy* (London, UK: Jossey-Bass, 2012), 19.

22. Mick Power and Tim Dalgleish, *Cognition and Emotion: From Order to Disorder* (London, UK: Psychology Press, 2015).

23. Cleveland Clinic, "Atychiphobia (Fear of Failure)," *Diseases & Conditions* (blog), Cleveland Clinic, accessed July 14, 2023, https://my.clevelandclinic.org/health/diseases/22555-atychiphobia-fear-of-failure.

24. Sara Blakely, "My Dad Demanded Failure," TheLeapTV, October 12, 2022, 00:01:35, https://www.youtube.com/watch?v=UjcyBQQdpCE.

25. Holly H. Brower, F. David Schoorman, and Hwee Hoon Tan, "A Model of Relational Leadership: The Integration of Trust and Leader-Member Exchange," *The Leadership Quarterly* 11, no. 2 (June 2000): 227–250, https://doi.org/10.1016/s1048-9843(00)00040-0.

26. Tim Boone, Anthony J. Reilly, and Marshall Sashkin, "Social Learning Theory," *Group & Organization Management*, 2, no. 3 (September 1977): 384–385, https://doi.org/10.1177/105960117700200317.

27. Alvin W. Gouldner, "The Norm of Reciprocity: A Preliminary Statement," *American Sociological Review* 25, no. 2 (April 1960): 161, https://doi.org/10.2307/2092623.

28. Practical Psychology, "Norm of Reciprocity (Definition + Examples)," *Practical Pie* (blog), October 8, 2023, https://practicalpie.com/norm-of-reciprocity/.

29. Peter M. Blau, *Exchange and Power in Social Life* (Oxfordshire, UK: Routledge eBooks, 2017), https://doi.org/10.4324/9780203792643.

30. Henri Tajfel and John Turner, "The Social Identity Theory of Intergroup Behavior," in *Political Psychology: Key Readings*, ed. J. T. Jost and J. Sidanius (East Sussex, UK: Psychology Press eBooks, 2004), 276–293, https://doi.org/10.4324/9780203505984-16.

Chapter 6

1. Tom Cox, "Organizational Healthiness: Work-Related Stress and Employee Health," in *Coping, Health, and Organizations*, ed. Philip Dewe, Michael Leiter, and Tom Cox (New York, NY: Taylor and Francis, 2000), 173–90.

2. Christopher Roussin, Tammy L. MacLean, and Jenny W. Rudolph, "The Safety in Unsafe Teams: A Multilevel Approach to Team Psychological Safety," *Journal of Management* 42, no. 6 (July 2016): 1409–1433, https://doi.org/10.1177/0149206314525204.

3. Dirk Van Dierendonck, "Servant Leadership: A Review and Synthesis," *Journal of Management* 37, no. 4 (September 2010): 1228–61, https://doi.org/10.1177/0149206310380462.

Chapter 7

1. Mikhail M. Bakhtin, "The Dialogic Imagination: Four Essays," trans. Caryl Emerson and Michael Holquist, *Slavic Review* 41, no. 3 (January 1982): 580–581, https://doi.org/10.2307/2497064.

2. North American Pet Health Insurance Association, "North American Pet Insurance Industry Surpasses $3.5 Billion-

NAPHIA," *News* (blog), *NAPHIA*, May 4, 2023, https://naphia.org/news/soi-report-2023/.

3. Lane Gillespie, *Bankrate's 2024 Annual Emergency Savings Report* (New York, NY: Bankrate, 2024), https://www.bankrate.com/banking/savings/emergency-savings-report/.

4. Walter Isaacson, *Steve Jobs* (New York, NY: Simon and Schuster, 2011).

5. Robert E. Quinn and John Rohrbaugh, "A Spatial Model of Effectiveness Criteria: Towards a Competing Values Approach to Organizational Analysis," *Management Science* 29, no. 3 (March 1983): 363–377, https://doi.org/10.1287/mnsc.29.3.363.

6. Elizabeth Wolfe Morrison and Frances J. Milliken, "Organizational Silence: A Barrier to Change and Development in a Pluralistic World," *The Academy of Management Review* 25, no. 4 (October 2000): 706, https://doi.org/10.2307/259200.

7. Christina G. Cataldo, Jonathan D. Raelin, and Melissa Lambert, "Reinvigorating the Struggling Organization: The Unification of Schein's Oeuvre into a Diagnostic Model," *The Journal of Applied Behavioral Science* 45, no. 1 (March 2009): 122–140, https://doi.org/10.1177/0021886308328849.

Chapter 8

1. Center for Creative Leadership, "How Leaders Can Build Psychological Safety at Work," *Leading Effectively* (blog),

Center for Creative Leadership, March 12, 2024, https://www.ccl.org/articles/leading-effectively-articles/what-is-psychological-safety-at-work/.

2. Bob Chapman, "Bob Chapman, Named Inc's #3 CEO in the World, Reflects on the Need for Caring Leaders," *News* (blog), Center for Positive Organizations, August 29, 2022, https://positiveorgs.bus.umich.edu/news/bob-chapman-named-incs-3-ceo-in-the-world-reflects-on-the-need-for-caring-leaders/.

3. Bob Chapman and Raj Sisodia, *Everybody Matters: The Extraordinary Power of Caring for Your People Like Family* (London, UK: Portfolio, 2015), 88.

4. Brent Stewart, "Building and Sustaining Company Culture with Rhonda Spencer," *Truly Human Leadership*, March 4, 2020, 00:36:05, https://www.barrywehmiller.com/post/podcast/2020/03/04/everybody-matters-podcast-rhonda-spencer-bw-chief-people-officer.

5. Enron Corporation, *Annual Report 1999* (Houston, TX: Enron Corporation, 1999), https://enroncorp.com/corp/investors/annuals/annual99/values.

6. Brent Stewart, "Building and Sustaining Company Culture with Rhonda Spencer," *Truly Human Leadership*, March 4, 2020, 00:36:05, https://www.barrywehmiller.com/post/podcast/2020/03/04/everybody-matters-podcast-rhonda-spencer-bw-chief-people-officer.

7. Dennis W. Organ, *Organizational Citizenship Behavior: The Good Soldier Syndrome* (Glencoe, IL: Free Press, 1988).

8. Brent Stewart, "Building and Sustaining Company Culture with Rhonda Spencer," *Truly Human Leadership*, March 4, 2020, 00:36:05, https://www.barrywehmiller.com/post/podcast/2020/03/04/everybody-matters-podcast-rhonda-spencer-bw-chief-people-officer.

9. Ibid.

10. Bob Chapman and Raj Sisodia, *Everybody Matters: The Extraordinary Power of Caring for Your People Like Family* (London, UK: Penguin UK, 2015), 88.

11. Ibid.

12. Barry-Wehmiller, "Chapman & Co. Leadership Institute and Leadership Alliance Combine to Create a Powerful Resource to Find, Develop and Retain Talent," *Barry-Wehmiller's Blog* (blog), December 15, 2021, https://www.barrywehmiller.com/news/company-news/release/chapman-co.-leadership-institute-and-leadership-alliance-combine-to-create-a-powerful-resource-to-find-develop-and-retain-talent.

13. Bob Chapman and Raj Sisodia, *Everybody Matters: The Extraordinary Power of Caring for Your People Like Family* (London, UK: Penguin UK, 2015).

14. Brent Stewart, "Building and Sustaining Company Culture with Rhonda Spencer," *Truly Human Leadership*, March 4, 2020, 00:36:05, https://www.barrywehmiller.com/post/podcast/2020/03/04/everybody-matters-podcast-rhonda-spencer-bw-chief-people-officer.

15. Bob Chapman, "How to Change Your Life in Three Days," *Barry-Wehmiller's Blog* (blog), February 13, 2013, https://www.barrywehmiller.com/post/blog/2020/03/06/how-to-change-your-life-in-three-days.

16. Bob Chapman and Raj Sisodia, *Everybody Matters: The Extraordinary Power of Caring for Your People Like Family* (London, UK: Penguin UK, 2015).

17. Ibid, 101.

18. Robert K. Greenleaf, *Servant Leadership: A Journey into the Nature of Legitimate Power and Greatness* (Mahwah, NJ: Paulist Press International, 1977), 27.

19. Jacob Stoller, *The Lean CEO: Leading the Way to World-Class Excellence* (New York, NY: McGraw-Hill, 2015), 172.

20. Barry-Wehmiller, "Kyle Chapman Olin Family Business Symposium," May 8, 2017, Vimeo, 00:07:26, https://vimeo.com/216514090.

21. BW Forsyth Partners, "Our Approach," Great Opportunities Begin with Great Partnerships, accessed July 15, 2024, https://www.bwforsyth.com/.

22. Barry-Wehmiller, "Our Acquisitions," Barry-Wehmiller, accessed July 17, 2024, https://www.barrywehmiller.com/story/acquisitions.

23. Bob Chapman and Raj Sisodia, *Everybody Matters: The Extraordinary Power of Caring for Your People Like Family* (London, UK: Penguin UK, 2015), 207.

Chapter 9

1. *Downfall: The Case Against Boeing*, directed by Rory Kennedy (2022; Netflix, 2022), 00:00:42, Netflix.

2. International Energy Agency, "World Air Passenger Traffic Evolution, 1980–2020—Charts—Data & Statistics—IEA," *Data* (blog), International Energy Agency, last updated December 3, 2020, https://www.iea.org/data-and-statistics/charts/world-air-passenger-traffic-evolution-1980-2020.

3. *Downfall: The Case Against Boeing*, directed by Rory Kennedy (2022; Netflix, 2022), 00:47:42, Netflix.

4. Boeing Media, "Boeing Changes Corporate Architecture to Support Growth and Value Strategies," March 21, 2001, https://boeing.mediaroom.com/2001-03-21-Boeing-Changes-Corporate-Architecture-to-Support-Growth-and-Value-Strategies.

5. Richard Robbins, "Hospitals, Aviation and Business," *Southwest Journal of Pulmonary, Critical Care and Sleep* 28 (February 2024): 20–23, https://doi.org/10.13175/swjpccs009-24.

6. *Airbus vs Boeing: The Jumbo Jet Race*, directed by Patrick Barberis (Indigenius, 2016), 00:26:26, YouTube.

7. David Schaper, "Boeing Employees Mocked FAA in Internal Messages before 737 Max Disasters," *Business* (blog), NPR, January 10, 2020, https://www.npr.org/2020/01/09/795123158/boeing-employees-mocked-faa-in-internal-messages-before-737-max-disasters.

8. *Downfall: The Case Against Boeing*, directed by Rory Kennedy (2022; Netflix, 2022), 00:01:50, Netflix.

9. Alan Boyle, "Investigation of Lion Air 737 Crash Focuses on Faulty Sensor: Why Wasn't It Fixed?" *GeekWire* (blog), November 28, 2018, https://www.geekwire.com/2018/lion-air-boeing-report/.

10. Peter Robison, "Boeing Built an Unsafe Plane, and Blamed the Pilots When It Crashed," *Irish Examiner*, December 27, 2021, https://www.irishexaminer.com/news/spotlight/arid-40772532.html.

11. Jon Hemmerdinger, "FAA 2018 Analysis Warned of 15 Fatal Max Crashes Months before Second Accident," *Safety (blog), Flight Global,* October 29, 2021, https://www.flightglobal.com/safety/faa-2018-analysis-warned-of-15-fatal-max-crashes-months-before-second-accident/135747.article.

12. US Senate Committee on Commerce, Science, and Transportation, *Committee Investigation Report—Aviation Safety Oversight* (Washington, DC: Commerce Committee Majority Staff, 2020), https://www.commerce.senate.gov/services/files/FFDA35FA-0442-465D-AC63-5634D9D3CEF6.

13. Tammy Duckworth Staff, "Duckworth Calls on FAA to Review Boeing's Disturbing Pattern of Failing to Disclose Critical 737 MAX Safety Information to Pilots | US Senator Tammy Duckworth of Illinois," April 4, 2024, https://www.duckworth.senate.gov/news/press-releases/duckworth-calls-on-faa-to-review-boeings-disturbing-pattern-of-failing-to-disclose-critical-737-max-safety-information-to-pilots.

14. Office of Public Affairs, "Boeing Charged with 737 Max Fraud Conspiracy and Agrees to Pay over $2.5 Billion," press release no. 21–17, January 7, 2021, https://www.justice.gov/opa/pr/boeing-charged-737-max-fraud-conspiracy-and-agrees-pay-over-25-billion.

15. Jeff Manning, "DeFazio Leads Congressional Charge Against Boeing, FAA," *Business* (blog), *OregonLive*, November 9, 2019, https://www.oregonlive.com/business/2019/11/defazio-leads-congressional-charge-against-boeing-faa.html.

16. David Schaper, "Boeing Employees Mocked FAA in Internal Messages before 737 Max Disasters," *Business* (blog), NPR, January 10, 2020, https://www.npr.org/2020/01/09/795123158/boeing-employees-mocked-faa-in-internal-messages-before-737-max-disasters.

17. Corporate Crime Reporter Staff, "Why Ed Pierson Won't Fly on a Boeing 737 MAX," *Corporate Crime Reporter* (blog), January 25, 2022, https://www.corporatecrimereporter.com/news/200/why-ed-pierson-will-not-fly-on-a-boeing-737-max/.

18. Ibid.

19. Cynthia McFadden, Anna Schecter, Kevin Monahan, and Rich Schapiro, "Former Boeing Manager Says He Warned Company of Problems Months before the 737 Max Crashes," *NBC News*, December 9, 2019, https://www.nbcnews.com/news/us-news/former-boeing-manager-says-he-warned-company-problems-prior-737-n1098536.

20. Ibid.

21. Joe Jacobsen, *Letter to Michael and Nadia Regarding Boeing 737 Max Design Flaws,* March 31, 2021, https://www.commerce.senate.gov/services/files/72283867-0DC7-40A9-82D6-D32C5ACD3C06.

22. Kai Ryssdal, "How Big Is Boeing's Slice of the GDP?" *Marketplace,* December 17, 2019, 00:28:57, https://www.marketplace.org/shows/marketplace/how-big-is-boeings-slice-of-the-gdp/.

23. Tom Hufty, "Faith at Work: An Interview with Dennis Muilenburg, CEO of the Boeing Company," *PointTaken,* October 3, 2018, 00:14:47, https://pointtaken.libsyn.com/episode-4-faith-at-work-an-interview-with-dennis-muilenburg-ceo-of-the-boeing-company.

24. Jon Smart, "Lack of Psychological Safety at Boeing," *IT Revolution* (blog), January 28, 2021, https://itrevolution.com/articles/lack-of-psychological-safety-at-boeing/.

25. Ethics Unwrapped Staff, "Ethical Fading," *Ethics Defined* (blog), *Ethics Unwrapped,* November 5, 2022, https://ethicsunwrapped.utexas.edu/glossary/ethical-fading.

26. *Flight/Risk,* directed by Omar Mullick and Karim Amer (2022; The Othrs) 1:30:52, Netflix.

27. Jon Smart, "Lack of Psychological Safety at Boeing," *IT Revolution* (blog), January 28, 2021, https://itrevolution.com/articles/lack-of-psychological-safety-at-boeing/.

28. Boeing Staff, "Our Values," *Sustainability* (blog), Boeing, accessed July 2, 2024, https://www.boeing.com/sustainability/values.

29. *Downfall: The Case Against Boeing*, directed by Rory Kennedy (2022; Netflix, 2022), 00:50:40, Netflix.

30. Ben Horowitz, *What You Do Is Who You Are: How to Create Your Business Culture* (London, UK: HarperCollins UK, 2019), 131.

Chapter 10

1. Thomas Gordon, *Parent Effectiveness Training: The "No-Lose" Program for Raising Responsible Children* (New York, NY: Plume Books, 1970).

2. Richard Rumelt, *Good Strategy Bad Strategy: The Difference and Why It Matters* (New York, NY: Crown Currency, 2011), 167.

3. Gretchen R. Vogelgesang, "How Leader Interactional Transparency Can Impact Follower Psychological Safety and Role Engagement," (PhD dissertation, University of Nebraska—Lincoln, 2007), https://digitalcommons.unl.edu/dissertations/AAI3291604.

4. Patrick M. Lencioni, *The Five Dysfunctions of a Team: A Leadership Fable*, 20th Anniversary Edition (Hoboken, NJ: John Wiley & Sons, 2010).

5. John Schaubroeck, Simon S. K. Lam, and Ann Peng, "Cognition-Based and Affect-Based Trust as Mediators of Leader Behavior Influences on Team Performance," *Journal of Applied Psychology* 96, no. 4 (January 2011): 863–71, https://doi.org/10.1037/a0022625.

6. Jennifer J. Kish-Gephart, James R. Detert, Linda Klebe Treviño, and Amy C. Edmondson, "Silenced by Fear: The Nature, Sources, and Consequences of Fear at Work," *Research in Organizational Behavior* 29 (January 2009): 163–93, https://doi.org/10.1016/j.riob.2009.07.002.

7. Linn Van Dyne and Jeffery A. LePine, "Helping and Voice Extra-Role Behaviors: Evidence of Construct and Predictive Validity," *The Academy of Management Journal* 41, no. 1 (February 1998): 108–19, https://doi.org/10.2307/256902.

8. Fred O. Walumbwa and John Schaubroeck, "Leader Personality Traits and Employee Voice Behavior: Mediating Roles of Ethical Leadership and Work Group Psychological Safety," *Journal of Applied Psychology* 94, no. 5 (January 2009): 1275–86, https://doi.org/10.1037/a0015848.

9. Jeffrey D. Ford and Laurie W. Ford, "Resistance to Change: A Reexamination and Extension," in *Research in Organizational Change and Development,* ed. Richard Woodman, William Pasmore, Rami Shani (Bingley, UK: Emerald Group Publishing Limited, 2009), 211–39, https://doi.org/10.1108/s0897-3016(2009)0000017008.

10. Amy C. Edmondson and Zhike Lei, "Psychological Safety: The History, Renaissance, and Future of an Interpersonal Construct," *Annual Review of Organizational Psychology and Organizational Behavior* 1, no. 1 (March 2014): 23–43, https://doi.org/10.1146/annurev-orgpsych-031413-091305.

11. Anonymous, *The Space Shuttle Challenger Disaster* (Charlottesville, VA: Online Ethics Center, 1992), https://

onlineethics.org/cases/engineering-ethics-cases-texas-am/
space-shuttle-challenger-disaster.

12. Michelle La Vone, "The Space Shuttle Challenger Disaster,"
    Space Disasters (blog), *Space Safety Magazine*, accessed
    August 16, 2024, https://www.spacesafetymagazine.com/
    space-disasters/challenger-disaster/.

13. Ibid.

14. John Hooker, "Professional Ethics: Does It Matter Which Hat
    We Wear?" *Journal of Business Ethics Education* 4 (2007): 103.

15. Michelle La Vone, "The Space Shuttle Challenger Disaster,"
    Space Disasters (blog), *Space Safety Magazine*, accessed
    August 16, 2024, https://www.spacesafetymagazine.com/
    space-disasters/challenger-disaster/.

16. William P. Rogers, "The Contributing Cause of the Accident," in
    *Report of the Presidential Commission the Space Shuttle Challenger
    Accident* (Washington, DC: Presidential Commission, 1986),
    https://www.nasa.gov/history/rogersrep/v1ch5.htm.

17. Ibid.

18. Mercury, "Deceased—Roger Boisjoly," *Philosophy
    of Science Portal* (blog), February 7, 2012, https://
    philosophyofscienceportal.blogspot.com/2012/02/deceased-
    roger-boisjoly.html.

19. William P. Rogers, "The Accident," in *Report of the
    Presidential Commission the Space Shuttle Challenger Accident*

(Washington, DC: Presidential Commission, 1986), https://www.nasa.gov/history/rogersrep/v1ch3.htm.

20. John Uri, "Thirty-Five Years Ago: Remembering Challenger and Her Crew," *History* (blog), NASA, January 28, 2021, https://www.nasa.gov/history/35-years-ago-remembering-challenger-and-her-crew/.

21. Guardian Staff Reporter, "'I Knew What Was about to Happen,'" *Science* (blog), *The Guardian*, February 14, 2018, https://www.theguardian.com/science/2001/jan/23/spaceexploration.g2.

22. Jessie Kratz, "'Roger, Go at Throttle Up:' The 35th Anniversary of the Space Shuttle Challenger Disaster," *Pieces of History* (blog), National Archives, December 13, 2021, https://prologue.blogs.archives.gov/2021/01/27/roger-go-at-throttle-up-the-35th-anniversary-of-the-space-shuttle-challenger-disaster/.

23. Star Dargin, "Stop Being Nice and Save Lives!," *Star Leadership's Blog* (blog), October 15, 2018, https://starleadership.com/stop-being-nice-and-save-lives/.

24. Jennifer J. Kish-Gephart, James R. Detert, Linda Klebe Treviño, and Amy C. Edmondson, "Silenced by Fear: The Nature, Sources, and Consequences of Fear at Work," *Research in Organizational Behavior* 29 (January 2009): 163–193, https://doi.org/10.1016/j.riob.2009.07.002.

25. Ibid.

26. Bennett J. Tepper, Jon C. Carr, Denise M. Breaux, Sharon Geider, Changya Hu, and Wei Hua, "Abusive Supervision,

Intentions to Quit, and Employees' Workplace Deviance: A Power/Dependence Analysis," *Organizational Behavior and Human Decision Processes* 109, no. 2 (July 2009): 156–167, https://doi.org/10.1016/j.obhdp.2009.03.004.

27. LaMarcus R. Bolton, Richard D. Harvey, Matthew J. Grawitch, and Larissa K. Barber, "Counterproductive Work Behaviours in Response to Emotional Exhaustion: A Moderated Mediational Approach," *Stress and Health* 28, no. 3 (October 2011): 222–233, https://doi.org/10.1002/smi.1425.

28. Thomas A. Wright and Stevan E. Hobfoll, "Commitment, Psychological Well-Being and Job Performance: An Examination of Conservation of Resources (Cor) Theory and Job Burnout," *Journal of Business & Management* 9, no. 4 (2004).

29. Howard Berkes, "Remembering Roger Boisjoly: He Tried to Stop Shuttle Challenger Launch," *The Two-Way* (blog), NPR, February 6, 2012, https://www.npr.org/sections/thetwo-way/2012/02/06/146490064/remembering-roger-boisjoly-he-tried-to-stop-shuttle-challenger-launch.

30. Ben Evans, "Missed Warnings: The Fatal Flaws Which Doomed Challenger Thirty-Two Years Ago (Part 2)," *Launch* (blog), *AmericaSpace*, January 30, 2018, https://www.americaspace.com/2018/01/30/missed-warnings-the-fatal-flaws-which-doomed-challenger-32-years-ago-part-2/.

31. Ronald A. Heifetz and Donald L. Laurie, "The Work of Leadership," *IEEE Engineering Management Review* 37, no. 3 (January 2009): 49–59, https://doi.org/10.1109/emr.2009.5235495.

32. James R. Detert and Ethan R. Burris, "Leadership Behavior and Employee Voice: Is the Door Really Open?" *The Academy of Management Journal* 50, no. 4 (August 2007): 869–884, https://doi.org/10.5465/amj.2007.26279183.

33. Ibid.

Chapter 11

1. Stephen Johnson, "Nine Out of Ten Americans Would Take a Pay Cut for More Meaningful Work," *Jobs and the Future of Work* (blog), World Economic Forum, November 8, 2018, https://www.weforum.org/agenda/2018/11/9-out-of-10-americans-would-take-a-pay-cut-for-more-meaningful-work/.

2. Jim Collins, "The Flywheel Effect," *Concepts* (blog), Jim Collins, accessed July 2, 2024, https://www.jimcollins.com/concepts/the-flywheel.html.

3. Frances Haugen, Statement of Frances Haugen, (Washington, DC: US Senate Committee on Commerce, Science and Transportation, 2021), https://www.commerce.senate.gov/services/files/FC8A558E-824E-4914-BEDB-3A7B1190BD49.

4. Robert Prentice, "A Whistleblower Faces Down Facebook," *From the Blog* (blog), *Ethics Unwrapped*, October 7, 2021, https://ethicsunwrapped.utexas.edu/a-whistleblower-faces-down-facebook.

5. Katie Bartlett, "Is a Too-Nice Workplace Culture of Ruinous Empathy Just as Damaging as a Toxic One?" *Radical*

Candor (blog), accessed October 13, 2023, https://www.radicalcandor.com/blog/culture-of-niceness/.

6. Lieutenant General David Morrison, "Leadership: Take a Stand, Make a Difference or Move On," Leadership and Team Learning, June 5, 2015, 00:03:06, https://www.youtube.com/watch?v=azbRhVCt8Rw.

7. Ibid.

8. Kimberly Brutsche and Tiarra McDaniel, "How Psychological Safety Creates Cohesion: A Leader's Guide," *The Army Resilience Directorate Newsletter*, April 2021, https://www.armyresilience.army.mil/ard/images/pdf/April%202021%20ARD%20Newsletter.pdf.

9. Ibid.

10. Kimberly Brutsche and Tiarra McDaniel, "How Psychological Safety Creates Cohesion: A Leader's Guide," *The Army Resilience Directorate Newsletter*, April 2021, https://www.armyresilience.army.mil/ard/images/pdf/April%202021%20ARD%20Newsletter.pdf.

11. Wang Hui, Anne S. Tsui, and Katherine Xin, "CEO Leadership Behaviors, Organizational Performance, and Employees' Attitudes," *The Leadership Quarterly* 22, no. 1 (February 2011): 92–105, https://doi.org/10.1016/j.leaqua.2010.12.009.

12. Kimberly B. Boal and Robert Hooijberg, "Strategic Leadership Research," *The Leadership Quarterly* 11, no. 4 (December 2000): 515–549, https://doi.org/10.1016/s1048-9843(00)00057-6.

13. Robert Eisenberger, Robin Huntington, Steven Hutchison, and Debora Sowa, "Perceived Organizational Support," *Journal of Applied Psychology* 71, no. 3 (August 1986): 500–507, https://doi.org/10.1037/0021-9010.71.3.500.

14. Barjinder Singh, Margaret A. Shaffer, and T.T. Selvarajan, "Antecedents of Organizational and Community Embeddedness: The Roles of Support, Psychological Safety, and Need to Belong," *Journal of Organizational Behavior* 39, no. 3 (September 2017): 339–354, https://doi.org/10.1002/job.2223.

15. Ibid.

16. Thrive Teaching Staff, "Mistakes We Make with Core Values: Meaningful or Meaningless?" *Thrive Teaching* (blog), September 15, 2023, https://thriveteaching.org/core-values/.

17. Patagonia (@patagonia), "For our 50th year, we're looking forward, not back, to life on Earth. Together, we can prioritize purpose over profit, collaboration over competition and protect this wondrous planet, our only home. What's next is unstoppable," X (formerly Twitter), March 10, 2023, https://x.com/patagonia/status/1634241652842741771.

18. Axios, "The 2023 Axios Harris Poll 100 Reputation Rankings," *Economy* (blog), *Axios*, May 23, 2023, https://www.axios.com/2023/05/23/corporate-brands-reputation-america.

19. Mark Zekoff, Kelsey Reddick, and Sarah Sawayda, *From the Outside in: Corporate Social Responsibility at Patagonia*, ed. O.C. Ferrell and Linda Ferrell (Auburn, AL: Auburn University, 2021),

https://harbert.auburn.edu/binaries/documents/center-for-ethical-organizational-cultures/cases/patagonia.pdf.

20. Kenji Explains, "'Don't Buy This Jacket'—Patagonia's Daring Campaign," *Better Marketing* (blog), November 15, 2022, https://bettermarketing.pub/dont-buy-this-jacket-patagonia-s-daring-campaign-2b37e145046b.

21. Evan Bush, "Patagonia Founder Gives Away Company, Ensuring Profits Go to Fight Climate Change," *Climate in Crisis* (blog), NBC News, September 14, 2022. https://www.nbcnews.com/science/environment/patagonia-founder-gives-company-away-ensuring-profits-go-fight-climate-rcna47793.

22. Lila MacLellan, "At Patagonia, Exit Interviews Are Rare—But They Go Deep," *Leadership* (blog), Quartz, March 20, 2019, https://qz.com/work/1574375/patagonias-hr-leader-has-been-moved-to-tears-in-exit-interviews.

23. Mercer Staff, "How Much Turnover Is Too Much?" *Mercer* (blog), September 21, 2023, https://www.imercer.com/articleinsights/workforce-turnover-trends.

24. Martha Beck, "Read an Excerpt from Martha Beck's New Book, *The Way of Integrity*," *Books* (blog) *Oprah Daily*, April 13, 2021, https://www.oprahdaily.com/entertainment/books/a36095680/martha-beck-way-of-integrity-excerpt/.

25. Will Marré, *Save the World and Still Be Home for Dinner: How to Create a Future of Sustainable Abundance for All* (Sterling, VA: Capital Books, 2009), 62.

26. Society for Human Resource Management Staff, "What Is Meant by 'Belonging' in the Workplace, and How Can It Be Measured?" *Q&A* (blog), Society for Human Resource Management, April 8, 2024, https://www.shrm.org/topics-tools/tools/hr-answers/meant-belonging-workplace-how-can-measured.

27. Amy C. Edmondson, *The Fearless Organization: Creating Psychological Safety in the Workplace for Learning, Innovation, and Growth* (Nashville, TN: John Wiley & Sons, 2018), 157.

Chapter 12

1. *Top Gun*, directed by Tony Scott (Paramount Pictures, 1986).

2. Richard M. Clark, *Developing Leaders of Character for the Twenty-First Century* (Air Force Academy, CO: United States Air Force Academy, 2021), https://www.usafa.edu/app/uploads/21st-Century-LoC-Final-March-2021.pdf.

3. United States Air Force Academy Center for Character and Leadership Development Faculty and Staff, "Developing Leaders of Character," *Leadership Overview* (blog), United States Air Force Academy, April 18, 2024, https://www.usafa.edu/character/.

4. Richard M. Clark, *Developing Leaders of Character for the Twenty-First Century* (Air Force Academy, CO: United States Air Force Academy, 2021), https://www.usafa.edu/app/uploads/21st-Century-LoC-Final-March-2021.pdf.

5. Bob Chapman and Raj Sisodia, *Everybody Matters: The Extraordinary Power of Caring for Your People Like Family* (London, UK: Portfolio, 2015), 77

6. Ibid.

7. J. Richard Hackman, "Why Teams Don't Work," interview by Diane Coutu, in *HBR's 10 Must Reads on Teams*, ed. *Havard Business Review* Staff (Brighton, MA: Harvard Business Publishing, 2013), 26.

8. Tom Geraghty, "Evolution of Leadership and Management in Healthcare: Lessons from Aviation and Crew Resource Management," *In Technology* (blog), *Psychological Safety Newsletter*, March 19, 2024, https://psychsafety.co.uk/the-evolution-of-leadership-and-management-in-healthcare-lessons-from-aviation-and-crew-resource-management/.

9. Simon Sinek, "The True Story behind *Leaders Eat Last*," Simon Sinek, August 23, 2023, 00:17:45, https://www.youtube.com/watch?v=FXzoZTwl_iI.

10. Ibid.

11. Simon Sinek, "Why Good Leaders Make You Feel Safe," March 2014, TED 2014, 00:11:45, https://www.ted.com/talks/simon_sinek_why_good_leaders_make_you_feel_safe/transcript?subtitle=en.

Chapter 13

1. Sam Haysom, "Stephen King Shares His Thoughts on AI Writing Fiction," *Entertainment* (blog), *Mashable*, August 24, 2023, https://mashable.com/article/stephen-king-ai-fiction.

2. George Orwell, *Nineteen Eighty-Four: The Graphic Novel* (London, UK: Penguin UK, 2021), 337.

3. Peter G. Northouse, *Introduction to Leadership: Concepts and Practice* (Thousand Oaks, CA: SAGE Publications, 2019), 7.

4. Suzanne Lucas, "Why Is Amazon Encouraging Recruiters to Resign?" *Evil HR Lady* (blog), December 14, 2022, https://www.evilhrlady.org/2022/12/why-is-amazon-encouraging-recruiters-to-resign.html.

5. Ibid.

6. Human Rights Watch, "Coalition Letter to Amazon Regarding the Facial Recognition System, Rekognition," *News* (blog), Human Rights Watch, October 28, 2020, https://www.hrw.org/news/2018/05/22/coalition-letter-amazon-regarding-facial-recognition-system-rekognition.

7. Spencer Soper, "Fired by Bot: 'It's You against the Machine,'" *Technology* (blog), *Bloomberg*, June 28, 2021, https://www.bloomberg.com/news/features/2021-06-28/fired-by-bot-amazon-turns-to-machine-managers-and-workers-are-losing-out.

8. Ryan Smith, "Leaked Amazon Memo Shows How It Forces out Employees to Hit Targets," *News* (blog), *Human Resources Director*, April 23, 2021, https://www.hcamag.com/us/news/general/leaked-amazon-memo-shows-how-it-forces-out-employees-to-hit-targets/253161.

9. UPS, "UPS to Enhance ORION With Continuous Delivery Route Optimization | About UPS," January 29, 2020, https://about.ups.com/us/en/newsroom/press-releases/innovation-driven/ups-to-enhance-orion-with-continuous-delivery-route-optimization.html.

10. UPS, "UPS to Mark World Environment Day by Matching Offsets of Carbon Neutral Shipments in June," July 1, 2020, https://about.ups.com/us/en/newsroom/press-releases/sustainable-services/ups-to-mark-world-environment-day-by-matching-offsets-of-carbon-neutral-shipments-in-june.html.

11. Linda Rhoades, Robert Eisenberger, and Stephen Armeli, "Affective Commitment to the Organization: The Contribution of Perceived Organizational Support," *Journal of Applied Psychology* 86, no. 5 (January 2001): 825–836, https://doi.org/10.1037/0021-9010.86.5.825.

12. Lisa Stovall, "The Unexpected Ways AI Is Boosting Employee Well-Being," *Employee Wellness Blog* (blog), *TotalWellness*, November 20, 2023, https://info.totalwellnesshealth.com/blog/ai-and-employee-well-being.

13. Hatim Rahman, "How Will AI Reshape Our World? It's Really up to Us," *Organizations* (blog), Kellogg School of Management at Northwestern University, January 17, 2024, https://insight.kellogg.northwestern.edu/article/how-will-ai-reshape-our-world.

14. Ibid.

15. Jordan Valinsky, "Bill Gates Explains How AI Will Change Our Lives in Five Years," *Finance* (blog), *Yahoo!*, January 16, 2024, https://ca.finance.yahoo.com/news/bill-gates-explains-ai-change-144546686.html.

16. James Manyika, "Google's SVP of Research, Technology, and Society: 'People Understand That AI Will Disrupt Their Lives—But They Hope It's for the Better. We

Must Not Let Them Down,'" *Rama on Healthcare* (blog), January 16, 2024, https://ramaonhealthcare.com/googles-svp-of-research-technology-and-society-people-understand-that-ai-will-disrupt-their-lives-but-they-hope-its-for-the-better-we-must-not-let-them-down/.

Conclusion

1. Office of the Assistant Secretary for Health (OASH), "U.S. Surgeon General Releases New Framework for Mental Health & Well-Being in the Workplace," October 20, 2022, https://www.hhs.gov/about/news/2022/10/20/us-surgeon-general-releases-new-framework-mental-health-well-being-workplace.html.

2. Addison Rizer, "Eight Psychological Safety Books," *Book Riot* (blog), November 15, 2023, https://bookriot.com/psychological-safety-books/.

3. Julia Rozovsky, *The Five Keys to a Successful Google Team* (Mountain View, CA: Google, 2015), https://www.michigan.gov/-/media/Project/Websites/mdhhs/Folder4/Folder10/Folder3/Folder110/Folder2/Folder210/Folder1/Folder310/Google-and-Psychological-Safety.pdf.

4. Ibid.

5. Julia Rozovsky, *The Five Keys to a Successful Google Team* (Mountain View, CA: Google, 2015), https://www.michigan.gov/-/media/Project/Websites/mdhhs/Folder4/Folder10/Folder3/Folder110/Folder2/Folder210/Folder1/Folder310/Google-and-Psychological-Safety.pdf.

6. Ibid.

7. Association of Executive Search and Leadership Consultants Staff, "The Top Reason for a Toxic Work Culture," *Insights* (blog), Association of Executive Search and Leadership Consultants, accessed August 16, 2024. https://www. aesc.org/insights/blog/business-leaders-believe-wrong-leadership-top-reason-toxic-work-culture.

8. Donald Sull, Charles Sull, and Ben Zweig, "Toxic Culture Is Driving the Great Resignation," *Measuring Culture* (blog), *MIT Sloan Management Review*, January 11, 2022, https:// sloanreview.mit.edu/article/toxic-culture-is-driving-the-great-resignation/.

9. Matt Poepsel, *Expand the Circle: Enlightened Leadership for Our New World of Work* (Washington, DC: New Degree Press, 2023), 11.

10. Douglas McGregor, *The Human Side of Enterprise* (New York, NY: McGraw-Hill, 1960).

11. Bruce J. Avolio, "Promoting More Integrative Strategies for Leadership Theory-Building," *The American Psychologist* 62, no. 1 (January 2007): 25–33, https://doi.org/10.1037/0003-066x.62.1.25.